HEBREWS

Beyond the Veil

JACK W. HAYFORD
Executive Editor

THOMAS NELSON
Since 1798

NASHVILLE   DALLAS   MEXICO CITY   RIO DE JANEIRO

Published in Nashville, Tennessee. Thomas Nelson is a registered trademark of Thomas Nelson, Inc.

Thomas Nelson, Inc., titles may be purchased in bulk for educational, business, fundraising, or sales promotional use. For information, please e-mail SpecialMarkets@ThomasNelson.com.

Unless otherwise indicated, all Scripture quotations are from the New King James Version, copyright © 1982 by Thomas Nelson, Inc.

Hayford, Jack W.

Hebrews: Beyond the Veil

ISBN 13: 978-1-4185-4121-7

Printed in the United States of America
09 10 11 12 13 14 — 6 5 4 3 2 1

TABLE OF CONTENTS

PREFACE

What Is "the Veil"?

IN THE OLD TESTAMENT, God dwelt in the Most Holy Place—that inner-most chamber of the temple. Between the chamber wherein the priests served (Holy Place) and the Most Holy Place hung a massive curtain, a veil, which symbolized the barrier of sin between God and man.

It was only on the Day of Atonement that anyone was allowed to pass beyond the veil and enter God's presence in the Most Holy Place. This annual day of sacrifice required that the high priest enter into God's presence from around the side of the veil; but he could not enter without bringing with him the blood of a sacrificial lamb. The blood of the sacrifice was sprinkled on the "mercy seat" (the altar within the Most Holy Place). Through this ritual, the sins of the people were "covered" for a period of one year. It was forbidden, on pain of death, for anyone to enter the Most Holy Place except the high priest on this one holy day each year. Only one man, once per year (an event that occurred by God's timetable, not man's desire), was allowed to venture beyond the veil.

But Jesus has brought us a better way! There is no longer any need for yearly animal sacrifice. He is the Lamb of God. His death is the eternal sacrifice and His blood has been sprinkled on the mercy seat of the kingdom of God. Our sins have been covered by His blood and through His sacrifice we are forgiven.

At the moment of Jesus' death, the veil of the temple was "torn in two from top to bottom" (Mark 15:38). The barrier between Holy God and sinful man was forever removed. Because of Jesus, we are granted free access into the very presence of God. Through Jesus Christ, our Lord and Savior, we have gained the right to "come boldly to the throne of grace" (Hebrews 4:16).

Keys of the Kingdom

K EYS CAN BE SYMBOLS of possession, of the right and ability to acquire, clarify, open, or ignite. Keys can be concepts that unleash mind-boggling possibilities. Keys clear the way to a possibility otherwise obstructed!

Jesus spoke of keys: "And I will give you the keys of the kingdom of heaven, and whatever you bind on earth will be bound in heaven, and whatever you loose on earth will be loosed in heaven" (Matthew 16:19).

While Jesus did not define the "keys" He has given, it is clear that He did confer upon His church specific tools that grant us access to a realm of spiritual "partnership" with Him. The "keys" are concepts or biblical themes, traceable throughout Scripture, that are verifiably dynamic when applied with solid faith under the lordship of Jesus Christ. The "partnership" is the essential feature of this enabling grace, allowing believers to receive Christ's promise of "kingdom keys," and to be assured of the Holy Spirit's readiness to actuate their power in the life of the believer.

Faithful students of the Word of God and some of today's most respected Christian leaders have noted some of the primary themes that undergird this spiritual partnership. A concise presentation of many of these primary themes can be found in the Kingdom Dynamics feature of *The New Spirit-Filled Life Bible.* The Spirit-Filled Life Study Guide series, an outgrowth of this Kingdom Dynamics feature, provides a treasury of more in-depth insights on these central truths. This study series offers challenges and insights designed to enable you to more readily understand and appropriate certain dynamic KINGDOM KEYS.

Each study guide has twelve to fourteen lessons, and a number of helpful features have been developed to assist you in your study, each marked by a symbol and heading for easy identification.

Kingdom Key

KINGDOM KEY identifies the foundational Scripture passage for each study session and highlights a basic concept or principle presented in the text along with cross-referenced passages.

Kingdom Life

The KINGDOM LIFE feature is designed to give practical understanding and insight. This feature will assist you in comprehending the truths contained in Scripture and applying them to your day-to-day needs, hurts, relationships, concerns, or circumstances.

Word Wealth

The WORD WEALTH feature provides important definitions of key terms.

Behind the Scenes

BEHIND THE SCENES supplies information about cultural beliefs and practices, doctrinal disputes, and various types of background information that will illuminate Bible passages and teachings.

Kingdom Extra

The optional KINGDOM EXTRA feature will guide you to Bible dictionaries, Bible encyclopedias, and other resources that will enable you to gain further insight into a given topic.

Probing the Depths

Finally, PROBING THE DEPTHS will present any controversial issues raised by particular lessons and cite Bible passages and other sources that will assist you in arriving at your own conclusions.

Each volume of the Spirit-Filled Life Study Guide series is a comprehensive resource presenting study and life-application questions and exercises with spaces provided for recording your answers. These study guides are designed to provide all you need to gain a good, basic understanding of the covered theme and apply biblical counsel to your life. You will need only a heart and mind open to the Holy Spirit, a prayerful attitude, a pencil, and a Bible to complete the studies and apply the truths they contain. However, you may want to have a notebook handy if you plan to expand your study to include the optional KINGDOM EXTRA feature.

The Bible study method used in this series employs four basic steps:

1. *Observation.* What does the text say?
2. *Interpretation.* What is the original meaning of the text?
3. *Correlation.* What light can be shed on this text by other Scripture passages?
4. *Application.* How should my life change in response to the Holy Spirit's teaching of this text?

The New King James Version is the translation used wherever Scripture portions are cited in the Spirit-Filled Life Study Guide series. Using this translation with this series will make your study easier, but it is certainly not imperative and you will profit through use of any translation you choose.

Through Bible study, you will grow in your essential understanding of the Lord, His kingdom, and your place in it; but you need more. Jesus was sent to teach us "all things" (John 14:25–26). Rely on the Holy Spirit to guide your study and your application of the Bible's truths. Bathe your study time in prayer as you use this series to learn of Him and His plan for your life. Ask the Spirit of God to illuminate the text, enlighten your mind, humble your will, and comfort your heart. And as you explore the Word of God and find the keys to unlock its riches, may the Holy Spirit fill every fiber of your being with the joy and power God longs to give all His children. Read diligently on. Stay open and submissive to Him. Learn to live your life as the Creator intended. You will not be disappointed. He promises you!

ADDITIONAL OBSERVATIONS

INTRODUCTION

Hebrews: Beyond the Veil

THE EPISTLE TO THE Hebrews is about Christ in His glory. The writer pulls together key insights about Jesus and His life on earth with a number of theological conclusions from the Old Testament concerning the preincarnate Christ and the ministry of Christ in glory today. The few but important references to Jesus "in the days of His flesh" (Hebrews 5:7) help us trust Him as One who intimately knows our human frailties, yet is not ashamed to call us His brothers (Hebrews 2:11)! The abundant Old Testament quotations and arguments portray Jesus as Son greater than Moses, the Conqueror greater than Joshua, and the Priest greater than Aaron. In all respects, Christ supersedes all! And His present ministry as intercessor for believers assures us that we shall persevere until we fully receive the "kingdom which cannot be shaken" (Hebrews 12:28).

The epistle to the Hebrews can be divided into three major thematic portions. Look up the following representative passages from each of the three portions and summarize their contents.

I. **The Superiority of Christ's Person (Hebrews 1:1—4:13)**
   Hebrews 2:5–9

II. **The Superiority of Christ's Works (Hebrews 4:14—10:18)**
   Hebrews 10:11–18

III. **The Superiority of the Walk of Faith (Hebrews 10:19—13:25)**
   Hebrews 12:1–4

An astonishing characteristic of the epistle to the Hebrews is a series of stern warnings that sometimes leave readers quaking in their spiritual boots. Summarize these warnings.

Hebrews 2:1–4

_____

_____

_____

Hebrews 3:12–15

_____

_____

_____

Hebrews 10:26–31

_____

_____

_____

Hebrews 12:25–29

_____

_____

_____

Although the writer of Hebrews issued such stern warnings to his readers, what was his basic attitude toward them (Hebrews 6:9–10)?

_____

_____

_____

What did the author pray for those who read his book (Hebrews 13:20–21)?

_____

_____

_____

The Author

The author of the epistle to the Hebrews is anonymous. The King James Version attributed the epistle to Paul, and some interpreters support this tradition. Because the Greek style is more classical than Paul's, other interpreters hypothesize that Paul wrote the epistle originally in Aramaic and that Luke translated it into Greek for a more general audience.

Still others reason from the polished style that the orator Apollos wrote Hebrews. (See Acts 18:24–28.) Priscilla is the candidate for authorship favored by some who suggest that a woman would have had reason to remain anonymous in first-century Jewish and Christian culture. Barnabas also has his supporters in the Who-Wrote-Hebrews Derby. Origen in the third century stated that "only God knows for certain who wrote Hebrews."

Basic Theme

The basic theme of Hebrews is found in the word *better,* describing the superiority of Christ in His person and work (1:4; 6:9; 7:7, 19, 22; 8:6; 9:23; 10:34; 11:16, 35, 40; 12:24). The words *perfect* and *heavenly* are also prominent. Christ offers a better revelation, position, priesthood, covenant, sacrifice, and power. The writer develops this theme to prevent the readers from giving up the substance for the shadow by abandoning Christianity and retreating into the old Jewish system. This epistle is also written to exhort them to become mature in Christ and to put away their spiritual dullness and degeneration. Thus, it stresses doctrine, particularly christology (the study of Christ) and soteriology (the study of salvation).

Background and Purpose

The majority of early Christians were Jewish. Apparently they expected Christ to return soon, but the delay in His coming and the persecutions against them caused them to wonder if they had made the right choice in becoming Christians. Consequently, they were in danger of returning to Judaism.

This epistle was written to the wavering Jewish believers, encouraging them to stand fast in their faith. The writer points out the overwhelming superiority of Christ over all that they had experienced under the law. The author dwells on the incomparable glory of the person and work of Christ.

Although Hebrews is specifically addressed to Jewish Christians, its teaching and practical admonitions are equally applicable to Gentile believers. In Christ there is no distinction between Jew and Gentile (Colossians 3:11). The church today needs the teaching provided in the Old Testament laws of worship that this book so beautifully relates to Christ and the gospel of eternal salvation. Christianity is not something added on to Judaism. It is something new, but a fuller understanding of the old covenant gives a richer and more marvelous appreciation of the new covenant of God's grace through our Lord Jesus Christ.

Prepare

Do you want to know what God is like? No one has ever seen Him; in fact, no one can look at God and live. However, God sent His Son into the world to make a sacrifice for the sins of humankind. In the time Jesus lived on earth, He demonstrated exactly what His Father is like. Then when the apostles explained the life and ministry of Jesus in the New Testament writings, they further clarified what the Father is like. The epistle to the Hebrews gives yet deeper insight into the nature of God, as no other book in the Bible, and points out the importance and the ministry of the preincarnate Christ.

Take the next week and read through the thirteen chapters of Hebrews. Read this letter seeking revelation from the Holy Spirit. Worship as you read, praising God and thanking Him for all He has done and for the greatness and superiority of who He is. Let the truth found in these pages cause you to look to Jesus, cause you to enter His presence boldly, without hesitation, and to honor and devote yourself to Him afresh.

SESSION ONE

The Best Revelation
Hebrews 1:1—2:18

Kingdom Key—*Behold Him*

John 1:14 The Word became flesh and dwelt among us, and we beheld His glory, the glory as of the only begotten of the Father, full of grace and truth.

The "glory of the Lord" was a term the Hebrews used to describe the way in which God showed that He was present through visible signs such as thunder, lightning, clouds, or fire (Exodus 3:1–6; 19:16–19; Numbers 12:5; 2 Chronicles 5:13–14). Jesus, being God, revealed to us all that God is. He fully showed forth the glory of God. Jesus is the eternal, ultimate expression of the Almighty, our Father God.

Read Psalm 19:1; Ephesians 1:12; Colossians 1:27; 1 Corinthians 6:19–20.

Questions:

What are two ways God reveals His glory?

_____

_____

Based on the way you live out your faith, what does your life tell others about the character of God?

_____

_____

By what means might you more effectively show forth the glory of God?

_____

_____

Kingdom Life—*Know His Excellency*

Hebrews 1:1–4 gives powerfully concise insight into the person and power of Jesus Christ. Read through these verses and list the seven excellencies (divine attributes or positions). Next to each, write what this truth means to you and how you can experience its power in your own life.

	Excellency	Personal Experience
1.		
2.		
3.		
4.		
5.		
6.		
7.		

Behind the Scenes

In Hebrews 1:6 Jesus is referred to as "the firstborn." Some view this as a reference to the incarnation, and others to the Second Coming. More likely, it refers to Christ's position of preeminence.

The position of firstborn son was of great import to the Hebrews. The firstborn son inherited special rights and privileges. His birthright was a double portion of the estate and leadership of the family. He was the family's spiritual head.

In figurative language the term *firstborn* stands for that which is most excellent. This expression is applied to Jesus in several New Testament passages. All of them point to Jesus' high standing and His unique relationship to His Father and the church.

Read Colossians 1:15–18; John 1:3; Romans 8:17, 29.

Questions:

What does it mean that you are a joint heir with Christ?

_____

_____

_____

In what ways should this impact your day-to-day life?

_____

_____

_____

Kingdom Extra

In both Hebrew and Greek the words translated "angel" mean "messenger." The author of Hebrews opened his epistle with an assertion that the Son was the greatest messenger about God. The balance of chapter 1 expands on the superiority of the Son to the angelic messengers.

The word translated as "spirits" in Hebrews 1:7 may also be translated "winds." Although angels occupy a high place as God's ministers, they are created. Therefore, they are as dependent and perishable as the forces of nature.

It is interesting that the writer contrasts the ministry of angels and the ministry of Christ. The ministry of Christ is eternal and His office is as divine Sovereign. Angels are but transitory beings whose office places them in service to both Christ and the saints. The similarity then is that of servant messenger.

A careful study will reveal that the activity of angels in the New Testament usually revolves around the ministry of Jesus and the establishment of His church on earth. They are ministering spirits or heavenly assistants who are continually active today in building the body of Christ, advancing the ministry of Jesus and the building of His church.

Word Wealth—*Ministers*

Ministers: Greek *leitourgos* (lie-toorg-oss'); Strong's *#3011*: From *laos,* "people," and *ergon,* "work"; hence, working for the people. The word first denoted someone who rendered public service at his own expense, then generally signified a public servant, a minister. In the New Testament it is used of earthly rulers (Romans 13:6); the apostle Paul (Romans 15:16); angels (Hebrews 1:7); and Christ (Hebrews 8:2).

Kingdom Life—*Much Is Required*

The writer to the Hebrews ventures far into the theological significance of the Old Testament and the person of the Son of God, but he never loses sight of the practical significance of learning spiritual truth. In Hebrews 2:1–4 the author issues the first of five stern warnings for his readers to act on the truth that they have received. (See 4:1–3, 11–13; 5:12—6:12; 10:19–39; 12:12–29.)

We are held accountable for what we know. This fact is echoed throughout the New Testament. It is imperative, if we are to serve as powerful disciples of Christ, that we cling to and act upon what we have learned.

We are also warned repeatedly about the dangers of allowing ourselves to drift due to complacency or sin.

Read Matthew 13:12; Luke 12:48; Hebrews 6:5–6; 1 John 4:17–19.

Questions:

What is the danger inherent in paying insufficient attention to divine revelation?

How does this first stern warning affect you?

How can you guard against complacency and drifting away?

What does a reaction of fear or dread reveal?

How can you guard against complacency and drifting away?

Kingdom Life—*Reinstated Dominion*

God has purposed men and not angels to be sovereigns of the created order. "The world to come" (Hebrews 2:5) is the new eternal order inaugurated by the enthronement of Christ, which is to be consummated at His return.

Instead of assuming his intended dominion over creation, man had become a slave, held in bondage by death and Satan.

So the eternal Son of God appeared in history on earth as Jesus the Man to provide a way of escape from bondage, access to God's presence, and an entrance into man's intended glory. Jesus the Man, exalted in glory at God's right hand, occupies the position of dominion intended for men, with everything put, or to be put, in subjection under His feet (Hebrews 2:8).

Through Him our dominion has been reinstated.

Read 2 Timothy 2:11–12; Revelation 5:10; 20:6; 22:5.

Questions:

What do you believe it means that we will rule and reign with Him?

How should the fact of your reinstated dominion change the way in which you live now?

✎ _____

_____

_____

Look up the meaning of the word *dominion* in a dictionary. Put into your own words what dominion in the life of a Christian should entail.

✎ _____

_____

_____

Kingdom Life—*Jesus Our Captain*

In Hebrews 2:10 the author emphasizes the genuine humanity of Jesus. The path that He trod as the suffering Redeemer was fitting, for thereby He was made perfect. This does not mean that Jesus had shortcomings that needed to be perfected, but that He became perfect or complete as an all-sufficient Savior. Only by suffering temptation and death did He qualify as our captain or leader who has gone ahead of us to open the way of salvation.

The word translated "captain" in Hebrews 2:10 is difficult to translate from the original Greek. The New King James Version translation "captain" emphasizes supremacy. The New Revised Standard Version translation "pioneer" captures the idea of participation. The New International Version translation "author" develops the idea of origination. Jesus originated salvation; He is the supreme Savior; and He gets personally involved with those being saved. The context of Hebrews 2 stresses the participatory aspect of the term.

Jesus Christ was the eternal Son of God, incarnate as a man—fully God and also fully and sinlessly human. The Father caused the Son to live for thirty-some years and die a shameful death so that He would be perfect, in the sense of being completed, as a Sanctifier.

We are Christ's brethren because in physical birth Jesus shares our descent from Adam, and in the new birth, believers become members of the family of God. There is a profound unity between Jesus and those He saves.

Read John 17.

Questions:

What do these passages tell you about the unity between you and Jesus?

_____

_____

Do you experience this sense of unity in your daily life?

_____

_____

_____

Why do you believe this is so?

_____

_____

What steps can you take to make this unity more of an experiential reality in your life?

_____

_____

_____

How can you find help in times of distress from the knowledge that Jesus stands with you in that distress?

_____

_____

_____

Behind the Scenes

Read Hebrews 2:11–12. This text quotes the messianic prophecy in Psalm 22:22, showing how the Spirit of the Christ fills the New Testament church and how Christ identifies Himself so closely with His people when they sing praises. As they do, two important things happen: (1) He joins in the song Himself, and (2) this joint praise releases the spirit of prophecy ("I will declare your name to My brethren"), as the holy power of praise ignites "the testimony of Jesus" (Revelation 19:10).

As we joyfully sing praise to our God, Christ comes to flood our minds with the glory of the Father's character ("name"). There is no doubt about it. The praises of the people in the church service release the spirit of prophetic revelation, the magnifying of God through Jesus Christ. Thus, praise introduces edification, exhortation, and comfort to bless the whole body.

Read Psalms 30:3–12; 61:8.

Questions:

Why are we repeatedly encouraged throughout Scripture to praise the Lord?

_____

_____

_____

What benefit do we receive through praise?

_____

_____

_____

How can you develop a lifestyle of praise?

_____

_____

_____

Probing the Depths

Man was created to live and breathe in an atmosphere of praise-filled worship to his Creator. The avenue of sustained inflow of divine power was to be kept by the sustained outflow of joyous and humble praise to his Maker. The severance of the bond of blessing-through-obedience that sin brought silenced man's praise-filled fellowship with God and introduced self-centeredness, self-pitying, and complaint.

(See Genesis 3:9–12.) But now salvation has come, and daily life in Christ calls us to prayer and the Word for fellowship and wisdom in living. Our daily approach to God in that communion is to be paved with praise: "Enter into His gates with thanksgiving, and into His courts with praise" (Psalm 100:4). Such a walk of praise-filled openness to Him will cultivate deep devotion, faithful obedience, and constant joy. Praise can bring steadfastness in godly living. A praise walk that is neither fanatical nor glib nor reduced to mere ritual will be a source of life-delivering power to those who freely give praise to God.

Read Psalms 42:5, 11; 43:5.

Questions:

What should be the correlation between praise and emotion?

How can you praise during times of suffering or want?

What do you believe would be the result of praising God when your life circumstance is negative?

Kingdom Life—*Free Indeed*

Jesus the perfect Man stood solidly alongside all humans. But He didn't become a man and suffer just to be an example that inspires and motivates people to live better lives. The suffering and death of Jesus was much more than an example. His death was a redemptive act that set believing people free from the power of sin and death.

The ultimate purpose of Christ's incarnation was the destruction of the Devil and deliverance from the fear of death (1 Corinthians 15:54–

57). The destruction of Satan does not mean that he is annihilated, but that his power is curbed in the lives of those committed to Christ.

Jesus became our High Priest. He provides our atonement ("at-one-ment" with God). He made the ultimate, once-and-for-all sacrifice that provides our salvation and freedom from sin and death. Since a high priest must be one with the people in order to represent them before God, the incarnation was indispensable to the atoning work of Jesus.

Read John 8:30–36.

Questions:

How do you experience the freedom of Christ in your daily life?

_____

_____

_____

_____

In what ways do you find you are still bound by Satan's schemes?

_____

_____

_____

How might you begin to experience freedom in these areas?

_____

_____

_____

_____

Behind the Scenes

The Devil is the main title for the angelic being who is the supreme enemy of God and man. Satan is his name, and devil is what he is—the accuser or deceiver. The title *Devil* appears thirty-five times in the New King James Version. In every case it is preceded by the article *the,* indicating a title rather than a name. The term comes from a Greek word that means a "false witness" or "malicious accuser."

The Devil is man's worst enemy (Matthew 13:25, 28, 38). This is the one enemy Jesus does not want us to love. He is an enemy of Christ, the church, and the gospel, and he is tireless in his efforts to uproot good and sow evil.

"He was a murderer from the beginning" (John 8:44) are the strong words from the lips of Jesus. The Devil killed Abel and the prophets, and he wanted to kill Jesus before His time (John 8:40).

Starting with Eve, the Devil has attempted to deceive every living soul (Revelation 20:10). Evil men operating under the power of the evil one will continue to deceive (2 Timothy 3:13).

Three times Jesus called the Devil "the ruler of this world" (John 12:31; 14:30; 16:11). The Devil offered the world to Jesus if He would worship him, but the Lord refused with these words, "Get behind Me, Satan" (Luke 4:8). At Calvary, God dealt a death blow to this world ruler. It is only a matter of time before God will win the final victory at the end of time (1 John 3:8; Matthew 25:41; Revelation 12:7).

The Devil is strong, but Christians are stronger through the Lord (Ephesians 6:11). The Devil tempts, but God provides a way of escape (1 Corinthians 10:13); the Devil tries to take advantage of people (2 Corinthians 2:11), but he will flee if fought (James 4:7). The Devil should not be feared, for Jesus is more powerful than this deceiving prince of the demons (1 John 4:4).

Word Wealth—*Propitiation*

Propitiation: Greek *hilasmos* (hil-as-moss'); Strong's #*2434*: Signifies an expiation, a means whereby sin is covered and remitted. To propitiate means to satisfy the wrath of God that has been justly and necessarily provoked by sin. It's a complicated concept that implies, on the one hand, that God's righteous wrath was directed against Jesus as the substitute for sinful people. On the other hand, propitiation requires the justification of those whose sins have been forgiven. Forgiven sinners must be given the righteousness of Jesus so that they can stand in the presence of God in His holiness. Propitiation does not change God's standards; it changes people to meet His standards.

Record Your Thoughts

Hebrews 2:18 says that Jesus "suffered, being tempted" and, on that basis, is able to sympathetically help you with your temptations.

Questions:

Do you think that the temptations Jesus experienced during His lifetime had much appeal to Him? Why or why not?

_____

_____

_____

_____

How powerful must His temptations have been for His experience to help Him understand your temptations?

_____

_____

_____

_____

What encouragement do you gain from knowing that Jesus became a perfect human being in order to die for sin?

_____

_____

_____

_____

What encouragement do you gain from knowing that Jesus gladly calls all Christians His brothers?

_____

_____

_____

_____

What encouragement do you gain from knowing that Jesus sets you free from sin and death?

_____

_____

_____

SESSION TWO

The Best Hope
Hebrews 3:1—4:13

Kingdom Key—*Find Peace with God*

Romans 5:1–2 Therefore, having been justified by faith, we have peace with God through our Lord Jesus Christ, through whom also we have access by faith into this grace in which we stand, and rejoice in hope of the glory of God.

True peace is more than the absence of strife or discord. It is a state of rest, quietness, and calmness, a sense of total well-being. This kind of peace comes only from knowing the Prince of Peace—Jesus, our Redeemer. The human heart longs for peace; Jesus promises it, and the Spirit longs to develop it.

The New Testament word for "peace" is *eirene*. It is a word that has its roots in the Old Testament *shalom,* which conveys the idea of well-being in all areas of life: health, wealth, success, and security. Although the degree to which some of the particulars of *shalom* comprise part of a New Testament life of *eirene* is subject to much debate, one thing is clear linguistically. Peace is something that touches every area of life.

True peace has to do with personal wholeness and beneficial relationships. It is an inward assurance that because we are positionally righteous with God by grace through faith in Jesus Christ, we have access to His powers to touch all facets of our lives. Hence, Hebrews 13:20–21 says, "Now may the God of peace . . . make you complete in every good work to do His will," so that life's relationships and circumstances reflect God's intent rather than that of selfish flesh.

Read Psalm 119:165; John 14:27; Romans 12:8; 1 Corinthians 7:15; 14:33; Philippians 4:7; Colossians 3:15.

Questions:

What things tend to cause you to lose your peace?

How can peace guard your heart and mind?

What lies at the root of peace with God?

How can you live in peace regardless of circumstance?

Kingdom Life—*Enter His Rest*

Throughout this section of Hebrews, we are given insight into the "rest" of God. This rest is entered when a believer fully trusts and places full confidence in God. The rest or peace of God is experienced in a life lived in right relationship to God, recognition of God's love and complete authority, and our own dependence upon and duty toward Him.

Read Psalms 16:8–11; 62:1–8; Isaiah 30:15.

Questions:

How have you experienced the soul rest of God?

_____

_____

_____

_____

How can this inner peace be made the norm instead of an isolated occurrence?

_____

_____

_____

_____

What effect would constant, continual soul rest have on your walk of faith? On your relationships within the kingdom?

_____

_____

_____

_____

Word Wealth—*Confession*

Confession: Greek *homologia* (hom-ol-og-ee′-ah); Strong's #*3671*: *Homologia* denotes "confession, by acknowledgment of the truth." It is comprised of the root words *homou,* meaning "the same" or "akin to," and *logos,* meaning the expression of a thought or conviction.

Kingdom Life—*Jesus Represents Us*

As an apostle, Christ is God's representative to His people. An apostle (Greek *apostolos*) is "one sent forth," an ambassador, a delegate, or a dedicated messenger. Jesus was sent to us to bring the good news of salvation through Him. He came to set up His church, to call together the people of the kingdom.

As High Priest, Jesus is our representative to God. Through His death He provided the work of atonement that covers our sins and reinstates our relationship with God. Unlike the atonement sacrifice of merely human high priests, which was repeated annually, this work was done once and for all time. His blood was shed to cover our sins, and He is our High Priest forever.

Read John 1:29.

Questions:

How do you experience Christ as an apostle or messenger in your own life?

_____

_____

_____

How do you experience Christ as your High Priest in daily life?

_____

_____

_____

How might continual awareness of His dual representative roles increase your effectiveness as an ambassador of His kingdom?

_____

_____

_____

In what ways are we to operate as both apostle and priest in our world? Support your answer with scriptural passages.

_____

_____

_____

Behind the Scenes

The writer of Hebrews extended his discussion of the superiority of the revelation of God in Christ to include Moses, the lawgiver, who was revered by Israel as the greatest man who ever lived. Earlier, the author had demonstrated that Jesus was superior to the angels who mediated the law. Next he focused on the superiority of Jesus as the receiver and recorder of the law.

Moses was the Hebrew prophet who delivered the Israelites from Egyptian slavery and who was their leader and lawgiver during their years of wandering in the wilderness. Moses was a leader so inspired by God that he was able to build a united nation from a race of oppressed and weary slaves. In the covenant ceremony at Mount Sinai, where the Ten Commandments were given, he founded the religious community known as Israel. As the interpreter of these covenant laws, he was the organizer of the community's religious and civil traditions. His story is told in the Old Testament in the books of Exodus, Leviticus, Numbers, and Deuteronomy.

After his death Moses continued to be viewed by Israel as the servant of the Lord (Joshua 1:1–2) and as the one through whom God spoke to Israel (Joshua 1:3; 8:24; 14:2). For that reason, although it was truly the law of God, the law given at Mount Sinai was consistently called the law of Moses (Joshua 1:7; 4:10).

The New Testament, however, shows that Moses' teaching was intended only to prepare humanity for the greater teaching and work of Jesus Christ. What Moses promised, Jesus fulfilled.

Read John 1:17; Romans 1:16—3:31.

Questions:

What does it mean to you personally that Jesus fulfilled the law?

How do you experience this benefit in daily life?

How might a greater recognition of this fact enable you to walk in rest and peace?

✎ _____

_____

_____

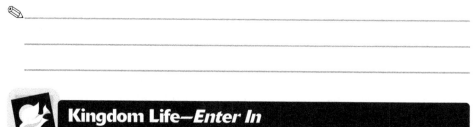

Kingdom Life—*Enter In*

Israel's failure to enter Canaan becomes a solemn warning in Hebrews 4:1. The rest promised us is not entrance into a place, but a state of being—a peace that passes understanding.

Some commentators view *rest* as a future heavenly reward. Others feel that the term describes the present experience of the believer who has fully surrendered to the lordship of Christ and is totally controlled by the Holy Spirit.

It is abundantly clear, however, that this rest hinges upon belief. Hearing the gospel does not have power to save; it is belief, acceptance, and confession that open the way for entrance into what God has prepared for those who love Him.

Read Mark 9:23–24; John 14:27; Romans 4:19–20; 10:17; Hebrews 3:12–15.

Questions:

With this in mind, what does it mean that "faith comes by hearing" (Romans 10:17)?

✎ _____

_____

_____

How can unbelief steal your rest or peace?

✎ _____

_____

_____

What steps can you take to increase your faith?

✎ _____

_____

Kingdom Life—*Members of the House*

Christ is worthy of more glory than Moses because Moses was merely a servant. Although the Jews revered him, Moses could only point the way to the Master's house, the promised land. Christ is both the builder and the Lord of the house. He is the fulfillment of all that Moses foreshadowed.

We are all members of the "household of faith" (Galatians 6:10), a term coined by Paul in his letter to the Galatian church. It is Christ who builds the house, and we dwell within its walls.

The house analogy continues in that we are also being built into worthy dwelling places for the Lord of all.

Read 1 Peter 2:4–8; Psalm 127:1.

Questions:

What does it mean to you to be part of the house that by inheritance belongs to Jesus? How should you feel and act because of that status?

✎ _____

_____

_____

How should this impact our experience in the community of believers?

✎ _____

_____

How have you experienced being built into a dwelling for the Lord?

✎ _____

_____

_____

What have been the results when you have taken this task of building upon yourself?

✎ _____

_____

Behind the Scenes

The writer of Hebrews testifies to the inspiration of the Old Testament by ascribing the quote from Psalm 95 (Hebrews 3:7–11) to the Holy Spirit. Using the tragic failure of the Israelites in the wilderness as an example, he solemnly warns his readers of the peril of unbelief. Their spirit of disobedience resulted in God's wrath, excluding them from entrance into the promised rest of Canaan.

Word Wealth—*Rest*

Rest: Greek *katapausis* (kat-ap'-ow-sis); Strong's #2663: The prefix *kata* suggests causation, and the root word *pauo* denotes a freedom from stress and/or effort. Combined here in the noun *katapausis,* the meaning is complete cessation of disquiet due to an external cause; in this case it is God who gives or withholds the rest.

Rest: Hebrew *menuchah* (meh-noo-chah'); Strong's #4496: This word carries the idea of soothing comfort. In Psalm 23:2 the divine Shepherd leads beside the waters of "rest." The name *Noah,* meaning "place of sanctuary," derives from this noun.

Kingdom Life—*Not of Works*

Works are those things we do, those tasks we accomplish. A subject of debate in biblical days as well as today, works are of importance but must be kept in proper perspective.

Just as God rested from His work of creation, the one who trusts in Christ rests in what God has done for him. He has ceased striving to achieve salvation by his own efforts, and in daily life has begun to learn a dependence upon the Holy Spirit.

However, we are held accountable for our actions in light of the truth we have gained. A faith that cannot be seen is not true faith. Read James 2:14–26.

Questions:

Restate the message of this passage in your own words.

_____

_____

_____

What message does your life give others about the reality of your faith?

_____

_____

_____

In what areas do you struggle to live out your faith?

_____

_____

What steps can you take to increase your life witness to others?

_____

_____

_____

Kingdom Life—*A Faithful Life*

Faith believes what God says and acts in line with His Word. Faith allows the believer to enter the rest into which God has called all His people. It acknowledges the completed work of salvation, while faithfully obeying every instruction from God.

Enter the rest promised by God. **Mix** your faith with God's Word. **Do not allow** rebellion to harden your heart. **Devote your whole heart** to obeying God and His Word. **Trust** Him to do the things He says He will do.

Behind the Scenes

Hebrews 4:11–13 is among the foremost scriptural passages that lead us to an understanding of faith's call to "confess" the Word of God. The lesson relates to

Israel's renunciation of God's promise, an act that resulted in a whole generation's dying in the wilderness and failing to possess the inheritance God intended for them.

In this context the Bible describes itself: "The word of God is living and powerful" (Hebrews 4:12). The term for "word" here is the Greek word *logos*, commonly indicating the expression of a complete idea and used in reference to the Holy Scriptures. It contrasts with *rhema*, generally used to refer to a word spoken or given. This recommends our understanding of the difference between *all* of the Bible and the *single* promise or promises the Holy Spirit may bring to mind from the Word of God.

When facing a situation of need, trial, or difficulty, the promises of God may become a *rhema* to you, a weapon of the Spirit. Its authority is that this "word" comes from the Bible—God's Word—the completed *logos*. Its immediate significance is that He has spoken it to your soul by His Spirit and is calling forth faith just as He did from Israel when He pointed them toward their inheritance.

Faith's confession received God's "words" (*rhema*) and stands firm upon these promises. However, faith's confession is strong not in human willpower, but in the divine will revealed in the whole of the Scriptures—the Holy Bible—the *logos* (completed Word) from which the *rhema* (present "word of promise") has been received.

Read Psalm 119:11–16; Proverbs 4:20–22; Ephesians 6:17.

Questions:

What are the benefits of hiding the Word of God in your heart?

✎_____

_____

_____

Do you place the appropriate degree of importance on reading, studying, meditating on, and memorizing God's Word? How so?

✎_____

_____

_____

How can the searching, revealing nature of God's Word assist you in more fully enjoying God's rest?

_____

_____

_____

_____

Record Your Thoughts

Questions:

How can reliance on the Word of God make your life more restful and peaceful?

_____

_____

_____

_____

How can reliance on the Spirit of God make your life more restful and peaceful?

_____

_____

_____

_____

What things in your life tend to disrupt the rest and peace God wants you to enjoy in Christ Jesus? How should you deal with them?

_____

_____

_____

_____

ADDITIONAL OBSERVATIONS

SESSION THREE

The Best Help

Hebrews 4:14—5:11

Philippians 4:19 My God shall supply all your need according to His riches in glory by Christ Jesus.

This verse tells us that God will supply our need by a distinct and definite measure, "according to His riches." In declaring this, God makes clear that He is not stingy when it comes to provision. His "riches" encompass all of creation, so there is nothing you need that He cannot provide! Do not misquote or misread this verse. It does not say that God shall supply your needs; it says that He shall supply your need. That includes everything at once, and all of it is adequately covered because He does it according to His riches. This verse cannot be lifted out of the Bible. It underwrites and relates to everything the Scriptures tell us to do in order to prosper. If we do what the Bible tells us to do, then God will provide abundantly.

The single most imperative provision God has made on our behalf is that of salvation. As with all things God provides, this gift is "according to His riches." It is a full salvation, a salvation overflowing with abundant provision for abundant life.

Read Zechariah 4:6; Matthew 6:25–34; Colossians 1:12–22; 1 Peter 5:7; 2 Peter 1:3–4.

Questions:

Make a list of the provisions you currently experience in the Lord.

✎ _____

_____

_____

Of what do you have need that you do not possess?

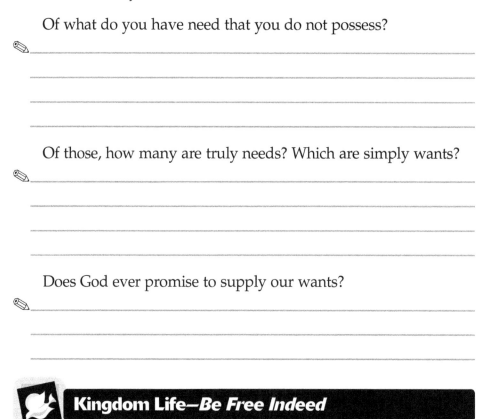

Of those, how many are truly needs? Which are simply wants?

Does God ever promise to supply our wants?

Kingdom Life—Be Free Indeed

Hebrews 4:14 concludes that Christians who recognize who Jesus is and what He has done will persevere in their confession of faith in Him. This is so because full recognition of Jesus' identity and purpose clarifies to the believing heart that He understands and is always able and available to supply all need encountered in a walk of faith.

The walk of faith is a glorious process of becoming increasingly free in Christ. By faith in Jesus' resurrection, we become free from the fear of death. Through faith in Jesus as our High Priest, we know that we have One who understands our temptations and can help us as we become free from sin. By faith in Jesus' holiness in our lives, we can be free to boldly enter God's presence without hesitation. We can come boldly and speak freely with our Father. We are free to come to God's throne of grace without reservation, with frankness, and with transparent honesty. There we receive mercy for the past and grace for the present and the future.

Read John 8:35–36; 2 Corinthians 3:17–18; Ephesians 1:15—2:7.

Questions:

What things of this world hold you bound?

_____

_____

_____

How might these Scripture passages lead you to find freedom?

_____

_____

_____

What does it mean to be in Jesus?

_____

_____

_____

What effect should this have on your daily walk of faith?

_____

_____

Kingdom Extra

The Greek word translated "to tempt" is a neutral term that can mean both "to test" in the way God proves the strength of our faith and "to tempt" in the way Satan appeals to us to sin. A particularly difficult circumstance is neutral. God desires to use it to prove the strength of character His Spirit has produced in us. Satan desires to use it to lure us to respond sinfully in obedience to the flesh. God views the incident as a trial; Satan intends the same incident as a temptation.

Read James 1:2–4, 12–16.

Questions:

What temptation do you most struggle with in your walk of faith?

_____

_____

How has this struggle affected your life?

_____

_____

_____

How can the insights offered in the above article help you withstand temptation?

_____

_____

_____

Behind the Scenes

The high priest was the supreme civil head of his people. Aaron held this position above his sons, and that was to continue in the firstborn of successive holders of the office. The high priest was distinguished from his fellow priests by the clothes he wore, the duties he performed, and the particular requirements placed upon him as the spiritual head of God's people.

Although the office of high priest was hereditary, its holder had to be without physical defect as well as holy in conduct (Leviticus 21:6–8). A high priest was consecrated (installed in office) by an elaborate seven-day service at the tabernacle or temple (Exodus 29; Leviticus 8). He was cleansed by bathing, dressed in the garments and symbols he must wear in his ministry, and anointed with special oil. Sacrifices of sin offerings, burnt offerings, and consecration offerings were made for him, and he was anointed again with oil and the blood of the sacrifice. Thus sanctified to serve as a priest and consecrated to offer sacrifice (Exodus 28:41; 29:9), he became "the saint [holy one] of the Lord" (Psalm 106:16).

The most important responsibility of the high priest was to conduct the service on the Day of Atonement, the tenth day of the seventh month of each year. On this day he alone entered the Holy Place inside the veil before God. Having made sacrifice for himself and for the people, he brought the blood into the Most Holy Place and sprinkled it on the mercy seat, God's throne, covering the sins of the people for the period of one year.

Kingdom Life—*Jesus Is Our High Priest*

Although Jesus perfectly fulfilled the requirements of high priesthood, the writer of Hebrews seems to have been concerned that his description of Jesus as a merciful high priest would not fit with his readers' preconceived ideas of a priest. The writer surveys the general characteristics required of a high priest in light of Jesus' fulfillment of each: He was appointed by God, He experienced genuine humanity, He made a sacrifice for sin "once for all" (Hebrews 7:27) when He offered Himself as the sacrifice, and He has an understanding sympathy for us. This last was perhaps the most critical high priestly characteristic as intercession requires an empathetic and compassionate heart.

Read Romans 8:34–39.

Questions:

What feelings are evoked by the knowledge that God the Son makes continual intercession on your behalf?

_____

_____

Do you consciously experience the unconditional understanding and empathetic love of Jesus in your daily walk? How so?

_____

_____

_____

What impact would the full realization of Jesus' compassionate heart have on your choices and reactions in day-to-day life?

_____

_____

What impact would this realization have on your relationships with others?

_____

_____

_____

Word Wealth—*Compassion*

Compassion: Greek *metriopatheo* (met-ree-op-ath-eh'-oh); Strong's #*3356*: This verb occurs nowhere else in the Bible. It means to control one's emotions because of extenuating circumstances. It conveys the idea of dealing gently, with consideration of another's limitations.

Probing the Depths

Hebrews 5:8 says of Jesus, "He learned obedience." This term carries the connotation of learning by repetition or practice. Jesus did not learn obedience in the sense that He did not initially understand the concept or agree with it. He learned obedience in the sense that an oft-repeated action will produce excellence and expertise. Jesus practiced obedience to the will of the Father until He became an artist of obedience.

Read Romans 2:5–10; Philippians 2:5–13.

Questions:

How might you more effectively practice obedience in your own life?

_____

_____

_____

How might this teaching affect your actions and attitudes when faced with life choices?

_____

_____

_____

In order to practice obedience, one must be aware of the will of the one obeyed. What actions can you take to begin hearing God's direction more clearly and know more certainly His will for you?

_____

_____

_____

What is the relationship between faith and obedience?

✎ _____

_____

_____

_____

Record Your Thoughts

Questions:

What spiritual burden have you cared enough about to offer it to God in prayers and supplications with tears?

✎ _____

_____

_____

_____

Read 2 Corinthians 10:3–5. What ideas ("arguments") or attitudes (things exalted "against the knowledge of God") related to this burden do you need to "cast down" by God's power in order to experience His victory in this matter? (See Jesus' own struggle in Matthew 26:36–42.)

✎ _____

_____

_____

_____

Compare Romans 12:1–2 and Hebrews 13:9–15. What sacrifices may we offer to God as a way of identifying with Jesus' sacrifice? How will our offering these sacrifices help us experience God's power through our burdens?

✎ _____

_____

_____

_____

What divine resource aids us beyond our own understanding as we pray (Romans 8:26)?

What spiritual discipline do you need to learn by disciplined repetition until it is second nature for you?

The Best Knowledge

Hebrews 5:12—6:20

Kingdom Key—*Embrace Understanding*

Proverbs 4:7–9 In all your getting, get understanding. Exalt her, and she will promote you; she will bring you honor, when you embrace her. She will place on your head an ornament of grace; a crown of glory she will deliver to you.

Just as Jesus practiced obedience, so we must learn the things of the kingdom by repetition and familiarization. This can happen only when we set out to acquire kingdom expertise through knowing God as He is revealed through His Son, His Word, and the Holy Spirit.

The natural learning process is realized by building upon a foundation of truth. Once a student has grasped the basics of a discipline, further and more complicated truth may be gained. But conscientious effort is required to reach a place of mature knowledge in any subject.

This is never truer than in the pursuit of maturity in the kingdom of God. When basic teachings of truth are not received and applied, there is no foundation for spiritual growth. Therefore, the more advanced teachings of the kingdom cannot be understood. It is imperative that those who desire to grow in the Lord apply themselves diligently to gaining knowledge and understanding.

Read Proverbs 4:4–13; 9:9–10; 23:12; 1 Corinthians 2:6–16; 2 Timothy 3:14–17; 1 Peter 2:2.

Questions:

Do you desire the Word of God in the same way an infant desires milk?

What will be the result of a life lived in pursuit of God's truth?

In what ways have you failed to build a strong foundation of faith? How can this be remedied?

Why do you think it is important that we recognize spiritual infancy in ourselves and be willing to admit our areas of immaturity?

Kingdom Life—*Build on the Basics*

In Hebrews 5:12 the writer uses the phrase "the first principles of the oracles of God." The Greek word used here means the very basics, the ABC's. The Hebrew Christians should have grown to be teachers, but they were still working on the spiritual alphabet.

The writer hoped to encourage the Hebrew believers to grow in their faith so that they could understand God's Word and plan and live out His will in their lives. These Hebrew believers most likely were familiar with Scripture, but the concern here is their grasp of its truth and their ability to apply it to the issues of life.

Read 1 Corinthians 3:1–3; Ephesians 4:14–16.

Questions:

What problems can result from immature faith?

What importance do you place on knowing the Word of God?

✎_____

_____

_____

When others look at your life, do they see maturity in the Lord? Why, or why not?

✎_____

_____

_____

What steps can you take to become a more mature believer?

✎_____

_____

_____

What happens to the personal lives of Christians who insist they are spiritually mature when, in fact, they are still children?

✎_____

_____

_____

What happens to immature Christians and their church when they assume leadership or teaching roles? (See James 3.)

✎_____

_____

_____

Word Wealth—*Partaker*

Partaker: Greek *metecho* (met-ekh'-oh); Strong's *#3348*: Literally "to have with." The word connotes a sharing in, participating with, copartnering or working in association with another, and taking part in a joint venture. In Hebrews 6:4 this refers to the indwelling and enablement of the Holy Spirit in the lives of those who have given themselves over to the lordship of Christ.

Probing the Depths

The important practical issue in Hebrews 6:6 is the meaning of "fall away." Can a believer fall away without knowing it in the course of backsliding, or must a believer decide to reject Christ even as he or she once chose to receive Him? What exactly is the writer attempting to communicate?

In order to more clearly understand this verse and its context, read the following paraphrase:

> True enough, you are immature as believers when I would expect you to be much more mature. But there's no point in my spending more time laying the foundation of your faith all over again; it's time for you to be up and growing unto maturity! Laying the foundation again would not help you one bit, nor would it help those who fully experienced salvation but then consciously, deliberately, and repeatedly disowned Christ and remain in that state to this day. Nothing can help them!
>
> And while you should be sobered by their state, the very fact that I am writing to help you shows my confidence that you (unlike them) will follow the example of the faithful and thus inherit all God's promises. Let's go on!

Hebrews acknowledges what each of us knows is true—genuine believers do sin (Hebrews 12:1), but without falling away. The act of falling away is not a matter of how often or of how many different ways one sins. "Falling away" in Hebrews refers to apostasy—the full, continuous denial of Christ as Lord and Savior by those who once trusted in and obeyed Him.

Behind the Scenes

The question is often asked: "If I sin, will I lose my salvation?" Let us look closely at the heart of this question and the reality of the answer.

Can you conceive of anyone adopting a child and then throwing her out on the street because she falls while learning to walk? When we are saved, we are adopted into the family of God. We must, out of love on one hand and godly fear on the other, seek to live a life that is pleasing to Him. But the idea that one act of sin would cause someone to be thrown out of God's family is not in the Bible (1 John 1:7, 9). However, acts of sin or rebellion will take away the joy of your salvation.

If one continues in a course of known sin, assurance of one's salvation may be lost, but that is not the same as an actual loss of one's salvation. A person born of the Spirit of God will always, at some point, be drawn back to repentance every time he sins.

Beyond that, we do read in Hebrews 10:29 that if someone actually says the blood of Jesus Christ is a common (unholy) thing and renounces the salvation he has received, then that person may have lost it all. But the same book says, "But, beloved, we are confident of better things concerning you" (Hebrews 6:9).

The loss of salvation to which Hebrews 6:4–6 refers is a complete disowning of Christ, a deliberate and decisive abandonment of the Christian faith. The people described are not backsliders but apostates. They have not merely fallen into sin, but have denounced Christ.

Read Isaiah 49:15–16; Joel 2:32; Matthew 28:20; Romans 10:8–13.

Questions:

Have you ever feared that you have lost your salvation?

_____

_____

_____

Why is this very fear an excellent indication that you have not?

_____

_____

_____

What promises do we have that make the loss of our salvation extremely improbable? Locate further Scriptures to support your answer.

_____

_____

_____

If salvation is lost, whose choice makes it so?

✎_____

_____

Kingdom Life—*Learn from Others*

In Hebrews 6:12 the writer encourages us "to imitate" those whose faith is strong, who live lives filled with faith in the One who promises, and hope that expects the things promised. "To imitate" carries a connotation of laziness and lack of originality to the modern mind. In the New Testament this word approximates the contemporary concepts of following a model or learning from a mentor. It was one of Paul's favorite expressions for learning from others.

Read 1 Corinthians 4:16; 11:1; Ephesians 5:1; Philippians 3:17; 1 Thessalonians 1:6; 2:14.

Questions:

Who are the ones the Lord has placed in your life from whom you can learn, whose lives you can imitate?

✎_____

_____

_____

What qualities do they possess that you desire in your own life?

✎_____

_____

Who are the ones who look to you as an example?

✎_____

_____

What does your life speak to them about the Lord and His kingdom?

✎_____

_____

_____

Word Wealth—*Patience*

Patience: Greek *makrothumia* (mak-roth-oo-mee'-ah); Strong's #*3115*: *Makrothumia* is from *"macros,"* meaning "long," and *thumos,* meaning "temper." Thus the word denotes lenience, forbearance, fortitude, patient endurance, longsuffering. This word also carries the idea of possessing the ability to endure persecution and ill-treatment. It describes a person who has the power to exercise revenge, but chooses to exercise restraint. This quality is a fruit of the Spirit (Galatians 5:22).

Kingdom Life—*Heirs of Promise*

As children of God, we should live in confident expectation of God's expressed purpose to bless us in Christ. The fulfillment of His promise to Abraham provides assurance that God will *always* perform what He promises. Therefore, we hope in and look forward to all that God has promised us through Christ.

Hope is a difficult biblical word because we associate wishfulness and indefiniteness with it. *Hope* in the Bible refers to something real but unseen. The realities of the spiritual world—such as God, angels, heaven, love, righteousness, peace, salvation—are foundational to the realities of the physical world. A biblical hope is more certain than the ground on which you stand. And "the blessed hope" (Titus 2:13), therefore, is the spiritual reality and certainty of the return of Christ. One of the things faith does is to enable us to comprehend and trust hope.

Read Psalms 16:8–11; 31:24; Romans 5:1–5; 8:23–25; 1 Peter 1:3–5.

Questions:

Why do you think all these references are forward-looking?

What can cause one to lose hope?

What happens to faith when one loses hope?

_____

_____

What does lack of hope say about one's concept of God and His love?

_____

_____

_____

Do you now, or have you ever, lacked hope? What was the result in your life and walk with the Lord?

_____

_____

_____

 **Kingdom Extra**

The concept of promise is vital to understanding the continuity of God's saving work through the Old Testament into the New Testament. The promise of a blessing made by God to Abraham and his descendants is the fundamental promise that all other biblical promises and covenants explain and expand (Genesis 12:2–3; Romans 9:6–8; Galatians 3:15–18; 4:28).

When the writer of Hebrews began to deal with persevering to the end and receiving the reward of a lifetime of mature discipleship, he naturally used the covenant phrase "inherit the promises" (Hebrews 6:12) and started using Abraham as the ultimate example of faith. From here to the end of Hebrews, "promises" or "the promise" refers to the benefits, blessings, and goals of salvation in Christ as the fulfillment of the new covenant (Hebrews 9:15; 10:36; 11:39–40).

Record Your Thoughts

Questions:

What promises of God do you go back to repeatedly as reference points for faith when you feel doubt creeping into your soul?

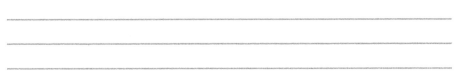

What do you feel that you have in common spiritually with Abraham, Moses, David, and other Old Testament recipients of promises?

Write a prayer of praise to the Lord Jesus in which you tell Him what it means to you that He anchors your soul in the presence of God.

ADDITIONAL OBSERVATIONS

SESSION FIVE

The Best Way

Hebrews 7:1–28

Kingdom Key—*Come to the Father*

John 14:6 Jesus said to him, "I am the way, the truth, and the life. No one comes to the Father except through Me."

The word *way* is indicative of a thoroughfare for travel, such as a path, road, or highway. Figuratively, the word *way* is used in the Old Testament as a synonym for God's divine will and manner of dealing with man (Psalm 1:6). In the New Testament the word is often used as a metaphor for man's moral course (Matthew 7:13–14; 2 Peter 2:15).

In the Old Testament the way to God was through the law. Under the new covenant the Way to God is Jesus. The purpose of all that Jesus did—the purpose of His life, His death, His resurrection—was to make a way for us to know God.

What a glorious truth, that our God longs for us to know Him. He desires it so deeply that He spared nothing, not even His only Son, to provide a way for us to enter into an intimate, loving relationship with Him.

Read John 3:16; 12:44–50; Romans 5:5–11; 1 John 4:7–16.

Questions:

In what ways do you find it difficult to have a close, loving relationship with the Father?

✎ _____

_____

_____

Is your relationship with Jesus closer than the one you have with the Father? Why do you believe this is so?

✎ _____

_____

_____

Behind the Scenes

Melchizedek was a king (of Jerusalem) and priest of the Most High God. His sudden appearance and disappearance in the book of Genesis are somewhat mysterious. In Genesis 14 we are told of Melchizedek's assistance to Abraham and his blessing upon Abraham.

Abraham presented Melchizedek with a tithe (a tenth) of his increase (through a recent battle victory). By this act Abraham indicated that he recognized Melchizedek as a fellow worshipper of the one true God as well as a priest who ranked higher spiritually than himself.

In Psalm 110, a messianic psalm written by David, Melchizedek is seen as a type of Christ. This theme is repeated in the book of Hebrews, where both Melchizedek and Christ are considered kings of righteousness and peace. By citing Melchizedek and his unique priesthood as a type, the writer shows that Christ's new priesthood is superior to the old Levitical order and the priesthood of Aaron (Hebrews 7:1–10).

Attempts have been made to identify Melchizedek as an imaginary character named Shem, an angel, the Holy Spirit, Christ, and others. All are products of speculation, not historical fact, and it is impossible to reconcile them with the theological argument of Hebrews. Melchizedek was a real, historical king-priest who served as a type for the greater King-Priest who was to come, Jesus Christ.

Kingdom Extra

A thousand years after the time of Abraham and a thousand years before the epistle to the Hebrews, David wrote Psalm 110 and made reference in verse 4 to the eternal priesthood of Melchizedek. Already, David was fascinated with the absence of detail about this great priest's lineage and his potential prophetic symbolism about the Messiah. Considering how much the writer of Hebrews makes of Psalm 110:4, it's interesting that no other New Testament writer picked up on the prophetic connection between Melchizedek and the Messiah.

Kingdom Life—*Our Priest Is Eternal*

We have seen that Melchizedek is a type of Christ. Like Melchizedek, Jesus Christ is a universal Priest and is at once both Priest and King. The silence concerning Melchizedek's ancestry, priestly pedigree, birth, and death illustrates the eternal and changeless priesthood of Christ.

Melchizedek represents a new, liberating priesthood that invites you and me to come directly to our glorious King and High Priest, Jesus Christ, with any problem or burden.

Read 1 Timothy 6:13–16; Revelation 19:16.

Questions:

What does it mean to you that Jesus is both your High Priest and your King?

In what ways do you fail to recognize Jesus as your eternal King?

How might full recognition of His rightful reign as King over your life change the way in which you relate to Him?

How might this recognition change the way you live out your faith?

✎ _____

_____

_____

Behind the Scenes

Levi was the third son of Jacob and Leah (Genesis 29:34). He was not an admirable man. Along with Simeon he massacred the inhabitants of Shechem in revenge for the rape of their sister Dinah (Genesis 34:25, 30). When Jacob blessed his sons before his death, he prophesied that Simeon and Levi would be scattered among the other tribes because of their cruel wrath (Genesis 49:5–7).

In time Moses and Aaron descended from Levi. Phinehas, a grandson of Aaron, halted a plague by acting ruthlessly for righteousness (Numbers 25:11–13). The Levites were scattered through Israel as priests in part because of Levi's cruelty and in part because of Phinehas's devotion to holiness. It's instructive that God chose a tribe in desperate need of forgiveness to represent Himself to the rest of the people.

Read Luke 7:36–47.

Questions:

What does God's choice of the Levites as His own special ministers say to you about God's capacity for love and forgiveness?

✎ _____

_____

_____

What impact should God's limitless mercy have on your day-to-day life?

✎ _____

_____

_____

_____

What more can you learn about God from His choice of the Levites?

✎ _____

_____

How might this realization affect your relationship with the Lord?

✎ _____

_____

Kingdom Extra

The word translated "perfect" indicates the final stage toward which a process is moving. Often "maturity" is a more accurate translation when the word is applied to finite humans. Look up the following uses of this term in the first seven chapters of Hebrews and summarize why the old priesthood and law were inadequate for perfection.

Read Hebrews 2:10; 5:9; 6:1, 19–20; 7:11–19.

Questions:

What is different about the new priesthood of the Lord Jesus in comparison with the Levitical priesthood?

✎ _____

_____

_____

What is different about the new promise of the Lord Jesus in comparison with the law of Moses?

✎ _____

_____

Compare Hebrews 7:19 with 6:19–20. Why do you think the new promises are called "a better hope, through which we draw near to God" (7:19)?

✎ _____

_____

How does the "better hope" impact your life today?

✎ _____

_____

What would you find the most distressing aspect of trying to keep the Mosaic law?

✎ _____

_____

When you think about the difficulties of Christian discipleship, what encouragement do you find in reflecting that you have promises based on "the power of an endless life" (7:16)?

✎ _____

_____

Word Wealth—*Make Intercession*

Make Intercession: Greek *entunchano* (en-toong-khan'-oh): Strong's #1793: To fall in with, meet with in order to converse. The meaning of this word progresses from a casual encounter to the idea of pleading with a person on behalf of another. In Romans 8:27 the Holy Spirit intercedes for the saints, and in verse 34 Christ is at the right hand of the Father interceding for believers. Both Spirit and Son continually engage the Father in conversation on our behalf.

Record Your Thoughts

The epistle to the Hebrews reveals just how carefully God constructed the Mosaic law and Levitical order of worship to prepare the way for redemption in Christ. Everything in some way illustrated an aspect of the spiritual reality Christ would make real.

Questions:

What has impressed you most so far about the use of the Old Testament by the writer of Hebrews?

✎ _____

_____

What comfort do you find in knowing that the Son of God is continually interceding on your behalf with the Father? What do you suppose He has been talking with God about for you?

✎ _____

_____

_____

_____

What insight does Jesus possess into your temptations as a result of being the High Priest who never yielded to temptation?

✎ _____

_____

_____

_____

In what ways and through what means does Jesus enable us to maintain victory over temptation?

✎ _____

_____

_____

_____

ADDITIONAL OBSERVATIONS

SESSION SIX

The Best Promise
Hebrews 8:1–13

✞ Kingdom Key—*Believe God*

2 Corinthians 1:20 All the promises of God in Him are Yes, and in Him Amen, to the glory of God through us.

Jesus Christ is the focus of our relationship with God. Jesus is God's "Yes" to us and our "Yes" to God. God came to us in Christ, reconciling the world to Himself through the new and everlasting covenant in Christ's blood. It is through this covenant that we have the promise of abundant, eternal life.

The first covenant was entirely external. It set a standard but provided no power to keep it. Under the new covenant there is complete, universal, and immediate knowledge of God. The promises of God toward us are made certain through Jesus Christ, our Savior, King, Priest, and Lord.

Read Galatians 3:13–14, 26–29; Ephesians 1:13–14; 1 John 2:24.

Questions:

What is God's most precious promise to you?

_____

_____

_____

What evidence is given that you have received the promise of God?

_____

_____

_____

In what ways is this evidence apparent in your life?

_____

_____

_____

How should the surety of this promise affect your life choices?

_____

_____

_____

Behind the Scenes

Old Testament priests always stood when they ministered in the early tabernacle and the later temple (Hebrews 10:11). There were no chairs among the furnishings of the Holy Place. The priestly work was never completed. It was always necessary for the priests to be available to offer still another sacrifice for sin.

Because Jesus offered one sacrifice at one point in time for all sins of all people in all times, He can sit down (Hebrews 1:3; 8:1; 10:12). Because He perfectly fulfilled the plans of the Father and has been exalted above all others, Christ is seated at the right hand of God. Because He initiated a new and better way to God after making the ultimate revelation of Him to humans, Christ is magnified with all of the majesty associated with the throne of God (Hebrews 8:1).

Read Ephesians 1:15—2:8; Romans 8:31–34.

Questions:

What does it mean to you that Christ is seated at God's right hand?

_____

_____

_____

How should this fact impact your relationship with God?

_____

_____

_____

How should this fact impact your daily life?

✎ _____

_____

_____

Kingdom Life—*All of Grace*

Grace is God's unmerited favor, a manifestation of His power far exceeding what we could ever hope to achieve by our own labors. Not only is grace mightily in effect in our salvation, it is also a God-given resource that makes holy living possible. God's grace becomes His enablement or empowerment to achieve His plan, endure hardship, or access Him. God's grace is powerful and all-enabling to the believer. It facilitates our abilities to conquer every weakness as we yield to an absolute reliance upon God, trusting His heart even when we cannot trace His hand.

We all live by either the principle of the law and our own man-made ideas of perfection or by God's principle of grace found in the New Testament. If we live by law, then it's all up to us to please Him by our efforts. But if we live by grace, we rely completely on God to make us pleasing to Him.

The book of Hebrews reminds us that God once used the law to prepare humankind to respond enthusiastically to grace.

Read John 1:14–17; Romans 3:21–24; 5:1–2, 20–21; 6:13–14; 11:6.

Questions:

What evidence of God's grace do you see in your own life?

✎ _____

_____

_____

In what ways do you attempt to gain God's favor by deeds or works?

✎ _____

_____

_____

When do you find it difficult to recognize God's grace at work in your life?

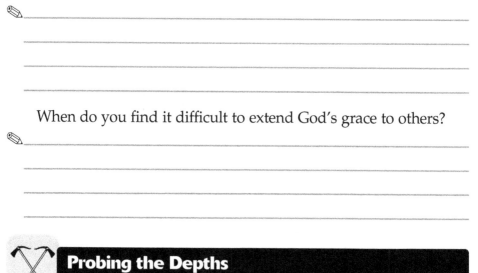

When do you find it difficult to extend God's grace to others?

Probing the Depths

Jesus' ministry is so superior to that of the Jewish priesthood that, by it, the old system is abolished and replaced by the absolute, eternal, and perfect priesthood of Christ.

The ministry of the tabernacle was only a type and symbol of the realities accomplished by Christ. Therefore, His ministry surpasses that of the Levitical priesthood as substance surpasses shadow. Jesus' ministry is performed in the true sanctuary of heaven. As Priest and King, He occupies the place of supreme power.

Sanctuary and *tabernacle* both refer to the heavenly presence of God. *Sanctuary* is to be understood as the inner room of the tabernacle where the ark of the covenant was kept. *Tabernacle* translates the common word for "tent," God's dwelling place during the years of Israel's wilderness wanderings.

Kingdom Extra

In Hebrews 8:5 the writer quoted Exodus 25:40 as evidence that God gave Moses exact directions for constructing the tabernacle and its furnishings. Read Exodus 25—27 for the complete tabernacle pattern the Lord revealed to Moses on Mount Sinai. Compare the instructions with the following illustrations.

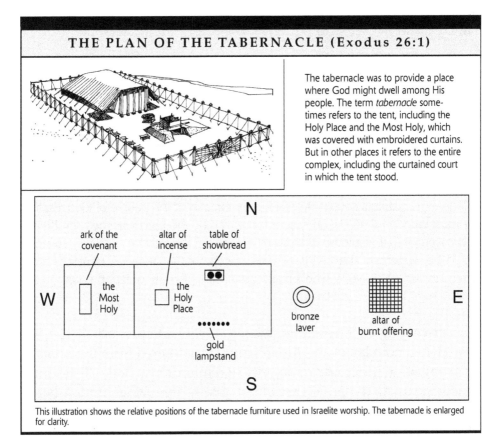

THE PLAN OF THE TABERNACLE (Exodus 26:1)

The tabernacle was to provide a place where God might dwell among His people. The term *tabernacle* sometimes refers to the tent, including the Holy Place and the Most Holy, which was covered with embroidered curtains. But in other places it refers to the entire complex, including the curtained court in which the tent stood.

N

ark of the covenant

altar of incense

table of showbread

W

the Most Holy

the Holy Place

bronze laver

altar of burnt offering

E

gold lampstand

S

This illustration shows the relative positions of the tabernacle furniture used in Israelite worship. The tabernacle is enlarged for clarity.

Word Wealth—*Mediator*

Mediator: Greek *mesites* (mes-ee'-tace); Strong's *#3316*: From *mesos,* meaning "middle," and *eimi,* meaning "to go"; hence, a go-between, umpire, reconciler, arbitrator, intermediary. This is a legal term denoting the role of Christ as the arbitrator between God and humanity. Hebrews goes to great lengths to demonstrate that Christ is fully God and fully human. In His person Christ brings God and humanity together. By means of His sacrifice for sins, He reconciles sinful humankind to holy God.

Probing the Depths

The two major passages in the Old Testament about the new covenant are Jeremiah 31:31–34 (the one quoted in Hebrews 8) and Ezekiel 36:25–27. Read these prophetic passages in their contexts and summarize the main provisions of the covenant.

✎ _____

_____

_____

_____

Behind the Scenes

The prophet Jeremiah ministered to the Southern Kingdom of Judah before, during, and after the final Babylonian conquest of Jerusalem. He witnessed the results of long-term, habitual covenant-breaking on the part of the people of God. Perhaps the most wonderful revelation granted Jeremiah by the Lord was the promise of a new covenant that would be radically different from the old one. This new covenant would be written on the hearts of God's people rather than on tablets of stone (Jeremiah 31:33). Anyone who breaks this covenant must violate the new nature given him or her by God Himself.

Jeremiah's vision was messianic. It looked forward to the end times when both Israel and Judah would be gathered from their dispersions, enjoying peace and prosperity (Jeremiah 30:1—31:30). It assumed a new spiritual dynamic capable of totally renewing human hearts (31:33). The epistle to the Hebrews provides the rest of the story.

Kingdom Life—*The Word of Life Within*

Jesus' ministry is performed under the covenant of God's grace, wrought within the minds and hearts of believers by the power of the Holy Spirit. Thus, God established a new, personal covenant relationship with His people. This new covenant is not based on a compelling force from without, as with the law; it is based on an impelling force from within—the Holy Spirit.

Read Romans 8:1–11.

Questions:

What is the most liberating aspect of the priestly ministry of Jesus Christ that frees you from bondage to the law?

✎ _____

_____

What confidence does it give you to know that you have a Mediator in heaven at the right hand of God?

✎ _____

_____

In what ways do you experience the impelling force of the Spirit of God?

✎ _____

_____

Record Your Thoughts

Questions:

How have you sensed in your Christian experience that the Spirit of God has written on your heart some part of the truth of God that changes you?

✎ _____

_____

What do you find most comforting and encouraging about the grace of God expressed in the new covenant?

✎ _____

_____

_____

In what ways have you experienced God's unmerited favor (grace) in your life?

✎ _____

_____

_____

Locate all the Scripture passages you can find that tell about God's grace. What new insight(s) have you gained?

✎ _____

_____

_____

ADDITIONAL OBSERVATIONS

SESSION SEVEN

The Best Cleansing

Hebrews 9:1–28

Kingdom Key—Be Purified

Revelation 1:5–6 To Him who loved us and washed us from our sins in His own blood, and has made us kings and priests to His God and Father, to Him be glory and dominion forever and ever. Amen.

The biblical distinction between "clean" and "unclean" has nothing to do with hygiene. Rather, it is the way God designated the difference between what He could receive into His presence and what must remain apart from Him.

Under the law only people, animals, and objects designated as clean could enter the tabernacle, and later the temple, as part of the worship of God. Specific rituals were instituted by God for making an unclean person or object clean. (See Leviticus 14; Isaiah 1:16.)

The designation of clean and unclean also implies a distinction between ethical character and behavior that is acceptable to God (holy) and that which is unacceptable (unholy). Jesus clearly taught that it is a person's character (heart) that determines whether or not he or she is clean and can be received into God's presence (Mark 7:15). Because of the spiritual nature of human character, external rituals cannot make anyone admissible to the Lord's presence. Only the blood of Jesus Christ can make us clean, and only through Him are we welcomed into the presence of God the Father (1 John 1:9).

Read Isaiah 1:18; 1 John 1:7–10; 3:1–3.

Questions:

Because of Jesus, you are clean before God. How should this fact affect your prayer life?

✎ _____

_____

_____

What other aspects of your life should be impacted by Jesus' provision of holiness in your life?

✎ _____

_____

Kingdom Life—*Purified by His Blood*

The writer of Hebrews has already reasoned that the earthly tabernacle Israel built in the wilderness at Mount Sinai symbolized heavenly realities about the presence of God. It follows logically that the sacrifices of the tabernacle also symbolized heavenly realities about atonement for sins.

The Bible attaches tremendous significance to the shedding of blood. Murderous bloodshed defiles the land in a way unparalleled by other sins (Genesis 4:10–11; 9:5–6; Numbers 35:33–34). By the same token, sacrificial bloodshed has purifying capability (Leviticus 16:11–19; 17:11; Hebrews 9:14, 22).

It was inevitable that the writer of Hebrews would come to this point: the blood of Christ provides a better purification from sins than the blood of sacrificial animals.

Read 1 John 1:7; Romans 5:12–21.

Questions:

Why do you believe God used the shedding of blood to purify from sin?

✎ _____

_____

What are the attributes of blood that make this a symbolic element to salvation?

✎ _____

_____

Probing the Depths

As you study the following illustration, consider the symbolism of each of the tabernacle furnishings and how it foreshadowed Christ.

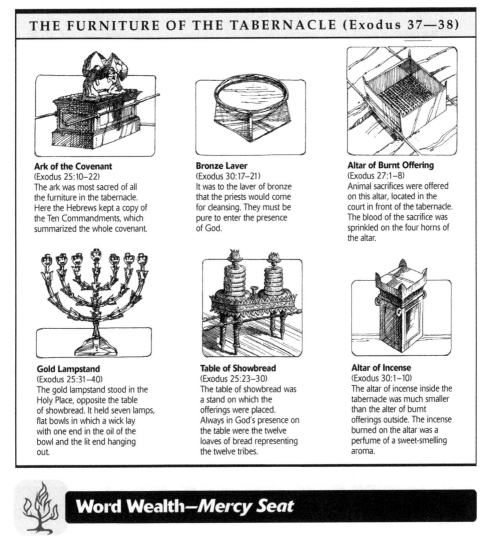

THE FURNITURE OF THE TABERNACLE (Exodus 37—38)

Ark of the Covenant
(Exodus 25:10–22)
The ark was most sacred of all the furniture in the tabernacle. Here the Hebrews kept a copy of the Ten Commandments, which summarized the whole covenant.

Bronze Laver
(Exodus 30:17–21)
It was to the laver of bronze that the priests would come for cleansing. They must be pure to enter the presence of God.

Altar of Burnt Offering
(Exodus 27:1–8)
Animal sacrifices were offered on this altar, located in the court in front of the tabernacle. The blood of the sacrifice was sprinkled on the four horns of the altar.

Gold Lampstand
(Exodus 25:31–40)
The gold lampstand stood in the Holy Place, opposite the table of showbread. It held seven lamps, flat bowls in which a wick lay with one end in the oil of the bowl and the lit end hanging out.

Table of Showbread
(Exodus 25:23–30)
The table of showbread was a stand on which the offerings were placed. Always in God's presence on the table were the twelve loaves of bread representing the twelve tribes.

Altar of Incense
(Exodus 30:1–10)
The altar of incense inside the tabernacle was much smaller than the alter of burnt offerings outside. The incense burned on the altar was a perfume of a sweet-smelling aroma.

Word Wealth—*Mercy Seat*

Mercy Seat: Greek *hilasterion* (hil-as-tay'-ree-on); Strong's #*2435*: Although used only in Hebrews and Romans 3:25 in the New Testament, the word is quite common in the Septuagint, where it primarily denotes the lid of gold above the ark of the covenant. It was upon this lid of gold that the Jewish high priest, in the ancient atonement ritual, would sprinkle the blood of the animal sacrifice to cover the sins of Israel. The root meaning of *hilasterion* is that of appeasing and placating an offended deity. Applied to the sacrifice of Christ, the word communicates that Christ's death was propitiatory, averting the wrath of God.

Behind the Scenes

The tenth day of the seventh month of the Hebrew calendar was set aside as the Day of Atonement, a day of public fasting and humiliation. On this day the nation of Israel sought atonement for its sins (Leviticus 23:27; 16:29–34; Numbers 29:7). This day fell in the month equivalent to our August, and it was preceded by special Sabbaths (Leviticus 23:24). The only fasting period required by the law (Leviticus 16:29; 23:31), the Day of Atonement was a recognition of man's inability to make an atonement for his sins. It was a solemn, holy day accompanied by elaborate ritual (Leviticus 16; Hebrews 10:1–10).

The high priest who officiated on this day first sanctified himself by taking a ceremonial bath and putting on white garments (Leviticus 16:4). Then he had to make atonement for himself and other priests by sacrificing a bullock (Leviticus 16:6). God dwelt on the mercy seat in the temple, but no person could approach it except through the mediation of the high priest who offered the blood of sacrifice.

After sacrificing a bullock, the high priest cast lots for a goat for a sin offering and a goat to be the scapegoat. After sacrificing the goat for the sin offering, he sprinkled its blood on and above the mercy seat (Leviticus 16:12, 14–15). Finally, the scapegoat bearing the sins of the people was sent into the wilderness (Leviticus 16:20–22). This scapegoat symbolized the pardon for sin brought through the sacrifice (Galatians 3:12; 2 Corinthians 5:21).

Word Wealth—*Conscience*

Conscience: Greek *suneidesis* (soon-i'-day-sis); Strong's #4893: Literally means "a knowing," a coknowledge with one's self, the witness borne to one's conduct by conscience, that faculty by which we apprehend the will of God as that which is designed to govern our lives. Conscience is the aspect of a human personality that evaluates the morality of a person's behavior.

Kingdom Life—*We Have Access to God*

The new covenant replaced the old one by fulfilling it. The new covenant brought to light the realities that the old one symbolized. There is no competition between the two covenants. The new one replaced the old one like a Christmas present replaces its picture in the catalog. The present satisfies all the longings its picture aroused.

In two verses the writer to the Hebrews quickly sketches the superior access to God provided through the high priestly ministry of Christ (Hebrews 9:11–12).

Questions:

What is superior about each of these aspects of the ministry of Christ?

The covenant

_____

_____

The tabernacle

_____

_____

Access to God

_____

_____

Redemption

_____

_____

 **Behind the Scenes**

The epistle of Hebrews contrasts the covenants of God through Moses and Christ. The Mosaic covenant provided animal sacrifices that brought temporary relief to man's guilt and demonstrated the lessons of God's justice. The covenant through

Moses provided a bond in the blood of animals. The sacrifices, however, had to be repeated annually at the tabernacle; the altar of the tabernacle was only symbolic of God's eternal, heavenly altar.

However, Jesus Christ came into history as an eternal Priest to offer an eternal sacrifice for sin. The shedding of His blood provided a permanent sacrifice and a permanent covenant between God and man. His blood was applied not merely to an earthly altar, but to the very altar of God in heaven, where once and for all it obtained redemption from sin for those who receive Him. The immutable bond that is established through the new covenant in Christ's blood is the ultimate fulfillment of God's covenant-making nature.

Read Psalm 111:9; Romans 11:26–27; 1 Corinthians 11:25.

Questions:

What is your understanding of covenant?

✎ _____

_____

_____

What does the act of entering into a covenant with man say of God's nature and purpose in the lives of men?

✎ _____

_____

_____

Locate scriptural and extrabiblical definitions and explanations of *covenant*. What further insight have you gained about God and His love for you?

✎ _____

_____

_____

 **Kingdom Extra**

The Greek language of New Testament times used one word, *diatheketo,* to cover the concepts we denote by the expressions "covenant" and "testament" (will).

One basic truth gives us tremendous insight into *diatheketo*: a will has no legal authority until after the death of the one who made it; it is ratified by the death of the author. In the same way, the death of Christ was necessary for the establishment of the new covenant.

Through His death He introduced the ideal system toward which the old sacrificial rituals pointed. Through His blood He provided what the blood of animals could only symbolize—a spiritual sacrifice to cleanse the soul. Without the shedding of Christ's blood, there is no forgiveness of sin. Under the new covenant our sin was carried away (as with the scapegoat under the law), and the blood of Christ was sprinkled on the mercy seat in heaven, eternally covering our sin.

The death of Christ fulfilled two distinct purposes: it provided atonement for past sins, and it provided an absolute ratification of the covenant with which it was connected.

Read Psalm 103:10–12; Romans 8:1–4.

Questions:

What do you believe is the difference between guilt and conviction?

_____

_____

_____

_____

Do you experience guilt over past sins?

_____

_____

With the previous Scripture portions in mind, what should be the appropriate response to guilt over sins of the past once they have been forgiven?

_____

_____

_____

_____

Word Wealth—*Remission*

Remission: Greek *aphesis* (af'-es-is); Strong's *#859:* From *aphiemi,* meaning to "send away." The word signifies a release from bondage or imprisonment, dismissal, and forgiveness, with the added quality of canceling out all judgment, punishment, obligation, or debt.

Kingdom Life—*Earth Is Only a Shadow*

Sometimes it is difficult to remember that our lives here are only a moment in time, a prelude to eternity. The things of this world steal our attention and impose their own importance.

However, the greater reality exists beyond the space and time in which we exist. The greater reality is spiritual. It is spiritual truth upon which all else is founded. It is the truth that gives meaning to all that is temporal.

The sacrifices of the old covenant were to teach of a greater spiritual reality—the complete adequacy of the sacrifice of Jesus. He entered into the limitations of the temporal to accomplish His eternal atoning work. Then He entered into heaven, opening for us the way of access to God.

He will one day return and gather to Himself those who, through faith in His atoning work, have entered into eternal life. We will then live with Him in a place beyond limitation. We will live with Him in the eternal kingdom of the Father.

Read John 3:16; 2 Corinthians 4:16–18.

Questions:

How would recognition of the transient nature of this life enable you to more fully live for God?

What steps could you take to allow this truth to become larger in your life?

✎_____

_____

_____

Record Your Thoughts

Write out as many promises as you can recall that God has guaranteed to you based on the covenant established by the death of Christ.

✎_____

_____

_____

_____

Questions:

In what ways do these promises affect your life today?

✎_____

_____

_____

_____

In what ways should these promises affect your relationships with others?

✎_____

_____

_____

_____

Write a psalm of praise to God for His wondrous grace.

✎_____

_____

_____

_____

ADDITIONAL OBSERVATIONS

SESSION EIGHT

The Best Sacrifice

Hebrews 10:1–18

Kingdom Key—*You Are Justified*

Isaiah 53:5 He was wounded for our transgressions, He was bruised for our iniquities; the chastisement for our peace was upon Him, and by His stripes we are healed.

The perfection of the sacrifice of Jesus Christ is not aesthetic. Humanly speaking, His death was a brutal execution. Divinely speaking, His death was a sacrifice for sin, an offering that satisfied God's justice and at the same time expressed His passionate love and mercy for all who would certainly be destroyed if God were only just and not also merciful.

When Ray Stedman was pastor of the Peninsula Bible Church in Palo Alto, California, he told the following story in a sermon based on the early verses of Hebrews 10:

> I remember growing up on the windswept plains of North Dakota. Sometimes the flames of a prairie fire would light the night horizon. Such prairie fires were terrible threats to the pioneers who crossed the plains in their covered wagons. Often these fires would burn for miles and miles, threatening everything in their path.
>
> When the pioneers saw such a fire coming toward them, driven before the wind, they employed a device to protect themselves. They would simply light another fire. The wind would catch it up and drive it on beyond them. Then they would get into the burned-over place and when the fire coming toward them reached it, it found nothing to burn and went out.
>
> God is saying that the cross of Jesus Christ is such a burned-over place. Those who trust in it, and rest in the judgment that has already been visited upon it, have no other judgment to face.

Read Romans 3:21–25; 5:6–11; 2 Corinthians 5:13–21.

Questions:

In what ways does being reconciled to God through Christ impact your daily life?

✎ _____

_____

_____

In what ways does the way you live your life speak to others of the reality of Christ's life, death, and resurrection?

✎ _____

_____

_____

You are now a "new creation" (2 Corinthians 5:17). How do you experience this truth in your life?

✎ _____

_____

_____

Behind the Scenes

It is interesting that the writer of Hebrews compared the old and new covenants to "shadow" and "image" rather than to "shadow" and "reality" (Hebrews 10:1). Historically, interpreters have understood the writer to be using an image from the world of first-century art. The "shadow" is the sketch or outline, the plan for the painting. The "image" is the completed masterpiece, with all of the details and brilliant colors in place.

Kingdom Life—Obedience Is Greater Than Sacrifice

In Hebrews 9 the writer showed how the annual Day of Atonement under the terms of the old covenant foreshadowed the more excellent way into the presence of God that Christ opened by means of His death. In chapter 10 the writer of Hebrews turned his attention to the way the various sacrifices of the old covenant picture the infinite self-sacrifice of God's Son.

The Levitical sacrifices of the Old Testament were repeated yearly. The constant repetition served as a continual reminder of sins but did not provide freedom from sin for the worshipper. These sacrifices, though ordained by God, were unsatisfactory because they were merely shadows and symbols of the new covenant in Christ's blood.

The fulfillment of God's will was set in motion by Christ's obedience: "I have come to do Your will, O God" (Hebrews 10:9).

Read 1 Samuel 15:22; Philippians 2:8–13.

Questions:

Why is obedience to God's will of primary importance?

_____

_____

What are the areas of your own life where rebellion exists?

_____

_____

What steps can you take to become more obedient to the will of God for your life?

_____

_____

_____

Behind the Scenes

Law is an orderly system of rules and regulations by which a society is governed. In the Bible, particularly the Old Testament, a unique law code was established by direct revelation from God to guide His people in their worship, in their relationship to Him, and in their social relationships with one another.

Israel was not the only nation to have a law code. The biblical law code, or the Mosaic law, was different from other ancient Near Eastern law codes in several ways. The biblical concept was that law comes from God, issues from His nature, and is holy, righteous, and good. At the outset of God's ruling over Israel at Sinai, God the Great King gave

His laws. These laws were binding on His people, and He upheld them. Furthermore, His laws were universal.

In Israel all crimes were crimes against God (1 Samuel 12:9–10). Consequently, He expected all His people to love and serve Him (Amos 5:21–24). As the final judge, He disciplined those who violated His law (Exodus 22:21–24; Deuteronomy 10:18). The nation or community was responsible for upholding the law and ensuring that justice was done (Deuteronomy 13:6–10; 17:7; Numbers 15:32–36).

Kingdom Extra

Several different types of offerings are specified by God throughout the Old Testament. These demonstrate human need and God's merciful provision.

The burnt offering involved a male animal wholly consumed by fire. The animal was killed and the priest collected the blood and sprinkled it about the altar (Numbers 28:1–8). The burning symbolized the worshipper's desire to be purged of sinful acts.

The meal offering, or grain offering, described in Leviticus 2, was similar in purpose to the burnt offering. The grain was brought to the priest, who threw a portion on the fire, accompanied by the burning of incense.

The peace offering was a ritual meal shared with God, the priests, and often other worshippers (Leviticus 3). A voluntary animal offering, the sacrifice expressed praise to God and fellowship with others.

The sin offering, also known as the guilt offering, was offered to make atonement for sins for which restitution was not possible (Leviticus 4:5–12).

The trespass offering was made for lesser or unintentional offenses for which restitution was possible (Leviticus 5:14–19).

Jesus is the Great High Priest who replaced the system of animal sacrifices with the once-for-all sacrifice of Himself.

Behind the Scenes

The writer of Hebrews quoted Psalm 40:6–8 from the Septuagint, the Greek Old Testament, which was widely used because most Jews were more familiar with

Greek than Hebrew. Read Psalm 40:6–8 and you discover that the second line says "My ears You have opened" instead of "But a body You have prepared for Me." The Septuagint translators seem to have interpreted David's words about his "ears" to mean that when his ears heard the truth about the true nature of sacrifices and offerings, he was ready to surrender his whole body in absolute, loving obedience. The open ears represented an obedient body.

The most logical conclusion to draw about the effect of a sacrifice characterized by a body yielded to the will of God is that people saved because of it should yield their bodies to the will of God.

Read Proverbs 20:12; Romans 10:17.

Questions:

In what way does having open ears allow you to more effectively serve the Lord?

In what area of your life do you find it difficult to hear the will of God?

In what area of your life do you find it difficult to hear the will of God?

What steps can you take to increase your ability to hear and understand God's will for your life?

Word Wealth—*Sanctified*

Sanctified: Greek *hagiazo* (hag-ee-ad'-zoe); Strong's #37: To hallow, set apart, dedicate, consecrate, separate, sanctify, make holy. In the Old Testament things, places, and ceremonies were named *hagiazo*. Sanctification is a major theological concept in the book of Hebrews. In the writings of Paul sanctification emphasizes the effect of the Holy Spirit on the character of a Christian. Here, however, sanctification is the effect of Christ's atonement. The sacrifice of Christ completely sets apart the redeemed person for God.

Read Ephesians 2:1–22; 2 Thessalonians 2:13.

Questions:

How does the blood of Jesus Christ relate to our being sanctified (being both purified and related directly to God for His work)?

_____

_____

_____

How does the Holy Spirit participate in our sanctification?

_____

_____

_____

Do you have a conscious experience of being set apart for service in your own life?

_____

_____

_____

Why do you believe this is so?

_____

_____

_____

How might full recognition of your sanctification through Christ impact your level of confidence and effectiveness in your life and ministry?

_____

_____

_____

Kingdom Life—*It Is Accomplished*

The use of the word *footstool* in Hebrews 10:13 creates a rich and important New Testament image based on Psalm 110:1. In the psalm David wrote, "The LORD said to my Lord, 'Sit at My right hand, till I make Your enemies Your footstool.'" Jesus referred to this verse as evidence of His deity (Matthew 22:41–45; Mark 12:35–37; Luke 20:41–44). Peter did the same thing in his pentecost sermon (Acts 2:34–36).

The writer of Hebrews used the reference to the footstool to highlight the idea that the work of Jesus is completed and He sits at rest (Hebrews 1:13; 10:1). In chapter 10 he added the idea of waiting at rest for a time when evil will be vanquished. The enemies of Christ will have to bow and let Him put His feet on their necks as their Conqueror. (See Joshua 10:24; 1 Kings 5:3.)

Kingdom Life—*Be Perfect*

Perfected is a repeated word in Hebrews. The basic meaning of the term is "mature" in the sense that a person has arrived at the condition of life intended for him or her by the will of God. In this sense Christ experienced perfecting through His earthly existence (Hebrews 2:10; 5:9; 7:28). Sinful humans can know perfecting only through the transforming work of the sacrifice of Christ (Hebrews 6:1; 7:11, 19; 9:9; 10:14). Perfection comes through a changed heart that surrenders its will totally to the Father so the person behaves as a living sacrifice.

Read Romans 12:1.

Questions:

In what way is Christ's sacrifice a model for us?

_____

_____

_____

In what ways can you live out Paul's entreaty to be a living sacrifice?

_____

_____

_____

What attitude lies at the heart of one who is a living sacrifice?

_____

_____

_____

Record Your Thoughts

Questions:

What are the biggest hindrances to the perfection of your life as a living sacrifice whose will is continually submitted to the Father?

_____

_____

_____

_____

What kingdom resources has God given you to overcome those hindrances (2 Peter 1:3–4)?

_____

_____

_____

_____

What assures us that God will continue transforming us unto Christ-likeness (Philippians 1:6; 2:13)?

_____

_____

_____

Locate and read the accounts of Christ's crucifixion in the Gospels. What aspect most impacts you at this point of our study?

_____

_____

_____

_____

The Best Assurance

Hebrews 10:19–39

Kingdom Key—*Have Confident Hope*

Romans 5:1–2 Therefore, having been justified by faith, we have peace with God through our Lord Jesus Christ, through whom also we have access by faith into this grace in which we stand, and rejoice in hope of the glory of God.

Throughout the pages of the New Testament, believers are encouraged to hold on to hope. We are to hope in Christ, not in the sense of an optimistic outlook or wishful thinking without any foundation, but in the sense of confident expectation based on solid certainty. Biblical hope rests on God's promises, particularly those pertaining to Christ's return. So certain is the future of the redeemed that the New Testament sometimes speaks of future events in the past tense, as though they were already accomplished. Hope is never inferior to faith, but is an extension of faith. Faith is the present possession of grace; hope is confidence in grace's future accomplishment.

Read 2 Corinthians 3:1–18; Titus 3:4–7; 1 Peter 1:3–21.

Questions:

What will be some of the resulting issues when one despairs of hope?

_____

_____

_____

What is true of one's faith when hope is lost?

_____

_____

_____

What has been provided by Christ to ensure hope remains alive in a seeking heart?

✎ _____

_____

_____

 Kingdom Life—*Draw Near*

Confidence to enter God's presence is founded on the blood of Jesus and His high priestly ministry. Because Jesus has opened the way for us through His sacrifice, we can boldly enter the very presence of God. Jesus is the living Way through whom you can draw near to God without hesitation, knowing you are welcome in His presence.

We can come confidently into God's presence when our approach is based upon an absolute assurance of the justifying power of the blood of Christ (Romans 5:1) and the sanctifying cleansing of the Word of God (Ephesians 5:26).

A true heart—a heart with complete sincerity of purpose—can only respond with pure worship in the presence of God.

Read Psalms 16:11; 95:1–6; 100:1–5; James 4:8.

Questions:

What does it mean that God will "draw near" (James 4:8) to you when you seek Him?

✎ _____

_____

What emotions are evoked in you when you consider standing in the presence of almighty God?

✎ _____

_____

What do these reactions reveal about your relationship with the Father?

✎ _____

_____

Kingdom Life—*Blessed Assurance*

The word translated as "assurance" in Hebrews 10:22 is the Greek *plerophoria* (play-rof-or-ee'-ah). At its root this word conveys the sense of absolute full measure or absolute fulfillment. To have *plerophoria* is to be filled with confidence to the uttermost. It is the engrossing effect of the expectation of the fulfillment of God's promises. It is the character of the faith by which we are to draw near to God.

The writer of Hebrews called on his readers to be assured of their salvation through active trust in Jesus Christ. Our assurance does not depend on the absence of struggle or the presence of warm, fuzzy feelings. Even in the face of struggle and difficulty associated with spiritual life and growth, we continue to trust. Assurance arises from carrying out the duties, avoiding the perils, and treasuring the memories of past spiritual experiences.

Read Psalms 37:3–5; 56:3–4; John 16:33; Ephesians 3:8–13.

Questions:

In what ways are assurance and trust intertwined in the heart of a believer?

✎ _____

_____

What is the relationship between peace and trust?

✎ _____

_____

In what ways are these three active in your life? Assurance? Trust? Peace?

✎ _____

_____

How can you work toward increasing the presence of each in your life?

✎ _____

_____

How can maintaining an active and vibrant daily relationship with Jesus Christ produce both the assurance of our salvation and the desire to perform our spiritual duties faithfully?

✎_____

_____

Behind the Scenes

"The Holiest" (Hebrews 10:19) was the most sacred inner room in the tabernacle and the temple where only the high priest was allowed to go. This room, separated from the rest of the worship area by a sacred veil, represented the visible presence of God in all His power and holiness. In this room was the ark of the covenant, covered by the sacred mercy seat (Exodus 25:10–22). Once a year on the Day of Atonement, the high priest entered the Most Holy Place (the Holiest) with sacrificial blood and made atonement before God for the sins of the people (Leviticus 16).

Read the following passages about the veil in the tabernacle, then summarize its significance for biblical worship.

| | Worship Significance | |
Passage	Literal	Symbolic
Exodus 26:31–33; 40:17–21	✎	
Leviticus 4:1–21	✎	
Numbers 4:5; 18:7	✎	
Matthew 27:50–54	✎	
Luke 23:44–49	✎	
2 Corinthians 3:7–18	✎	
Hebrews 6:19–20; 9:1–4; 10:20	✎	

Probing the Depths

In the few words of Hebrews 10:26 is one of the most solemn, fearful warnings of Scripture. If one willfully forsakes Christ, there is no other sacrifice for sin.

It is imperative here that we understand the difference between doubt (even severe), backsliding, and apostasy. The very struggle involved with battling doubt suggests the choice to believe has been made. The recognition of a backslidden state reveals a heart attuned to its duty toward God and convicted of its failure. Both these states, while unhealthy, are proof of salvation, while an apostate heart has rejected God.

Apostasy is a willful, defiant attitude that denies the Son of God and counts His sacrifice as worthless. It is to treat the Son of God with scorn and contempt. An apostate heart knowingly rejects the Spirit of grace, denying Father, Son, and Spirit even after having personally experienced their presence.

Question:

How would you distinguish doubt—even extreme doubt—from deliberate apostasy?

_____

_____

_____

Behind the Scenes

The writer of Hebrews had a particular scenario of apostasy in mind as he wrote his epistle. It would appear that the Jewish Christians to whom he wrote were considering reverting to the practice of Judaism in the face of persecution and ostracism by the larger Jewish community in which they lived. That is why the writer went to such trouble to develop biblical arguments for the temporary nature of the old covenant. The new covenant in Christ is not just preferable. It has fulfilled and replaced the old. One cannot go back without renouncing the only basis for the forgiveness of sins and eternal life.

Read Romans 6:4–14; Ephesians 4:17–24; John 1:16–17.

Questions:

What does it mean to be made new?

_____

_____

_____

Once a person has become new, how can he or she return to the old?

_____

_____

_____

In what way does grace provide for sin in a Christian's life?

_____

_____

_____

In what ways might Satan deceive a Christian to the point that he or she would renounce Christ?

_____

_____

_____

Spiritual indifference and backsliding on the part of Christians are not the same thing as apostasy. How could these conditions put one in danger of choosing to apostatize?

_____

_____

_____

What do you suppose would need to happen in a person's heart and mind before they could apostatize?

_____

_____

_____

Word Wealth—*Illuminated*

Illuminated: Greek *photizo* (fo-tid′-zo); Strong's #*5461*: From the root *phos*, meaning "to give light" and, metaphorically, "reaching the mind." *Photizo* also appears in Hebrews 6:4 where it is translated as "enlightened." The image pictures the moment when the truth of Christ was apprehended by the human mind and spirit and accepted by faith. That moment of insight and faith was like a light being lit. The same moment of conversion is described in Hebrews 10:26 with the expression "received the knowledge of the truth."

Kingdom Life—*Persevere*

Perseverance is the biblical term used to describe Christians who faithfully endure and remain steadfast in the face of opposition, attack, and discouragement. Those who focus on Jesus can bear up under any load. Perseverance involves *patience*— the ability to endure without complaint and with calmness. Perseverance also includes *persistence* in accomplishing goals and *permanence* for a lifetime of commitment.

Christians are to persevere in prayer (Ephesians 6:18), in faith (Hebrews 12:1–2), in obedience (Revelation 14:12), and in service (1 Corinthians 15:58). As believers commit themselves daily to godly living, they are abundantly rewarded by the Lord with the fruit of His Spirit for all eternity. Daily recommitment leads to lasting discipline.

The world is not comfortable with commitment. Promises are easily broken and contracts are frequently altered. The children of God are called to a life of commitment to God and to each other. To faith, virtue, and knowledge, the believer is required to add self-control and perseverance. The promise is that those who endure and persevere in overcoming evil will be greatly rewarded with God's blessings both now and in eternity.

Read Galatians 5:22–25; Romans 5:3–5; James 1:2–4; 2 Peter 1:5–7; 2 Timothy 3:10–14.

Questions:

How does the fruit of the Spirit enable us to walk in perseverance?

Is this fruit in evidence in your life?

_____

_____

How might you grow more mature in this area of your life?

_____

_____

_____

What benefits might a greater degree of perseverance add to your personal life? Your ministry? Your walk with the Lord?

_____

_____

_____

Word Wealth—*Endurance*

Endurance: Greek *hupomone* (hoop-om-on-ay'); Strong's #*5281*: Constancy, perseverance, continuance, bearing up, steadfastness, holding out, patient endurance. The word combines *hupo,* meaning "under," and *mone,* meaning "to remain." It describes the capacity to continue to bear up under difficult circumstances, not with a passive complacency but with a hopeful fortitude that actively resists weariness and defeat.

Record Your Thoughts

Even as Jesus persevered in doing the will of God, so believers in Jesus also need to persevere. We must remember all of God's past mercies in the midst of present trial and never fail to look forward to the imminent return of the Lord.

Questions:

At what points in your past do you recall God's hand at work in the midst of trial?

_____

_____

_____

What was the effect on your faith?

How do those memories motivate you to endure today?

How do those memories add to your assurance of salvation?

ADDITIONAL OBSERVATIONS

SESSION TEN

The Best Faith

Hebrews 11:1–40

Kingdom Key—*Only Believe*

Romans 1:16–17 I am not ashamed of the gospel of Christ, for it is the power of God to salvation for everyone who believes, for the Jew first and also for the Greek. For in it the righteousness of God is revealed from faith to faith; as it is written, "The just shall live by faith."

"The just shall live by faith." These six little words have life-changing, mind-altering power. In them we find the soul of the Christian faith.

These words were first spoken by the Old Testament prophet Habakkuk. The Lord gave Habakkuk an unpleasant task. He got to tell the nation of Judah that they were so wicked God was going to punish them by means of the Babylonians, a brutal, godless nation of people. Habakkuk was convinced that God had made a moral error in deciding to punish the bad by means of the worse and told Him so. When the Lord failed to change His mind, Habakkuk did some serious soul-searching.

As a result of his inner struggle, Habakkuk reached a staggering conclusion, a conclusion that shaped all the theology of Paul and later the theology of the Reformation.

Read Habakkuk 2:4; Romans 4:5; Ephesians 2:8; 2 Corinthians 1:24; 5:7; 1 John 5:4–5.

Questions:

In what way does living by faith open the way for a heart filled with joy?

✎ _____

_____

What is God's reaction to faith in the life of a believer?

_____

_____

What is the fruit of faith in the life of a believer?

_____

_____

How does one live by faith?

_____

_____

Kingdom Life—*Faith Works*

The first seven verses of Hebrews 11 describe faith and illustrate how faith in God and His Word provides a basic framework for understanding and dealing with reality.

"Now faith is the substance of things hoped for, the evidence of things not seen" (Hebrews 11:1) should not be understood as a definition of faith but as a description of how faith works. An established conviction concerning things not (yet) visible will result in the settled expectation of future reward.

The Greek word translated "substance" literally means "a standing under" and carries the idea of a foundation or basis for claim. It was used in the technical sense of a title deed. The word *evidence* contains the idea of a test or proof. Thus, the root idea is that of standing under the claim to a property to support its validity. Faith is the title deed "of things hoped for." It is the absolute assurance of possessing what God has promised.

Questions:

How do you think faith provides a test or proof "of things not seen" (11:1)?

_____

_____

_____

What do you think is the difference in meaning between "things hoped for" and "things not seen" (11:1)?

_____

_____

When has this faith (assurance of God's promises) been in evidence in your own life?

_____

_____

What impact did this have on your attitude and ability to withstand trial?

_____

_____

Why do you think God values your faith more than any other attitude you can direct toward Him?

_____

_____

Kingdom Extra

In order to understand what faith is, it will be of value to understand what faith is not. Though we may hear much to lead us to believe faith is a kind of positive thinking, no mental attitude will bring change to any aspect of our lives except ourselves. Faith is not hoping for the best, it is not optimism, nor is it a gut feeling that all will be well.

Faith is the recognition that reality exists beyond what we can discern through our five senses. Reality exists in God, and faith reaches toward Him for truth. Faith believes God and adjusts life (actions, thoughts, responses) to the promises He has made.

This faith is seen in "the elders" (Hebrews 11:2), the Old Testament saints, who are mentioned in this faith chapter of Hebrews. They obtained a good report, not because of achievements, personal holiness, or passive acceptance of divine promises, but by an active certitude expressed in obedience, persistence, and sacrifice. We would do well to follow their example.

Read Genesis 1:1—2:24; 4:1–15; 5:19–24; 6:9—9:1.

Questions:

What aspects of faith's role in grasping reality are illustrated by each of these Old Testament incidents?

✎ _____

_____

_____

Creation (Hebrews 11:3)

✎ _____

_____

Abel's sacrifice (Hebrews 11:4)

✎ _____

_____

Enoch's translation (Hebrews 11:5–6)

✎ _____

_____

Noah's ark (Hebrews 11:7)

✎ _____

_____

Kingdom Life—*Faith Is Personal*

It is when faith turns from foundational issues of reality to personal issues of salvation that we find out whether we trust God to make and keep His promises. It's one thing to believe that God has established a physical, moral, and spiritual order in the universe. It's another matter to believe that He wants to direct your life and still another for you to let Him direct your life.

Read Psalm 37:3–5; Romans 4:20; 2 Corinthians 1:18–21.

Questions:

What role does trust play in living a life of faith?

✎ _____

_____

What prevents you from fully trusting the Lord and His promises?

✎ _____

_____

What would be some personal benefits of walking by faith?

✎ _____

_____

With these Scriptures in mind, why is it impossible to please God without faith?

✎ _____

_____

Behind the Scenes

Hebrews 11 records glorious victories of faith's champions, yet verses 13–16 speak of those who died "not having received the promises" (v. 13). Even then, the Bible says "these all died in faith" (v. 13), being content to confess that they were only strangers and pilgrims traveling, as it were, through the land. Whether in life or in death, their faith remained strong for it was founded in the Lord, not on circumstance.

The key to the confession of this admirable group in Hebrews 11 is that when given a promise by God, as were Abraham and his descendants, they became fully persuaded that the promise was true. Thus they embraced (literally "greeted") that promise in their hearts. The word *confess* helps us to understand how easily these of the gallery of faith established their ways before God and left the testimony that His Word records with tribute.

While each of these persons did receive *many* victories through faith, the text says that none of them received *everything* that was promised. Although they received only a partial fulfillment of what God had promised, these elders maintained their faith that God would do what He said. Because of their close relationship with God, they could not feel at home in earthly surroundings. They looked for something better; because of their longings, God gladly acknowledged them as His own people.

Whether or not we receive what we confess (ask, pray, or hope for) does not change the behavior or attitude of the steadfast believer. Faith's worship and walk do not depend on answered or unanswered prayers. Our confession of His lordship in our lives is to be consistent— a daily celebration with deep gratitude.

Read Psalms 7:17; 42:11.

Questions:

Does seemingly unanswered prayer negatively impact your faith?

_____

_____

What is your reaction when you do not receive what you prayed for?

_____

_____

Do you continue in an attitude of praise when your desires are not met? Why do you believe this is so?

_____

_____

What methods could you employ to grow in this area?

_____

_____

Word Wealth—*Heir/Promise*

Heir: Greek *sunkleronomos* (soong-klay-ron-om'-oss); Strong's #4789: From *sun,* meaning "with," *klero,* meaning "a lot," and *nemomai,* meaning "to possess." The word denotes a joint participant, coheir, fellow heir, one who receives a lot with another.

Promise: Greek *epangelia* (ep-ang-el-ee'-ah); Strong's #*1860*: Both a promise and the thing promised, an announcement with the special sense of promise, pledge, and offer. *Epangelia* tells what the promise of God is and then gives the assurance that the thing promised will be done.

This word differs by only one letter from the word translated "gospel" (*euangelia*). While the "gospel" is a good and pleasant announcement from God, the "promise" is a sure and certain announcement from God. In Hebrews the promise is synonymous with the new covenant or testament by which people of faith inherit the purification of sanctification. The promise is established through the high priestly ministry of Jesus on the basis of His once-for-all sacrifice of Himself for sins.

Kingdom Life—*Faith Focuses on God*

The starting place of faith is the realization of what is real. The goal is grasping the promises of God that bring His blessings to bear on the believer's life. Faith is the basis for all victories in the conflicts and conquests of the spiritual life. Faith allows us to flee confidently to God when in trouble and to abide in Him for protection.

Faith is a forward focus on God, His Word, and His promises, remembering the past blessings of God to gain strength in order to face the future with endurance and gain its reward.

Read Psalms 62:5–8; 91:1–2; 103:1–5; Proverbs 3:19–26.

Questions:

What experiences of your past increase your faith today?

_____

_____

What are the benefits of God in your own life?

_____

_____

How can recalling these strengthen your walk of faith?

_____

_____

What steps can you take to more effectively grasp the promises of God?

✎ _____

_____

Behind the Scenes

If Moses had remained in the court of Pharaoh rather than identifying with the people of Israel, he would have become a man of great worldly power. He had received the finest education of the day and demonstrated unusual ability as an orator and leader (Acts 7:22). In time Moses would have distinguished himself as a well-known man in the mightiest empire of the world—and been lost in the obscurity of history.

Instead, Moses regarded such a choice as sin against the will of God (Hebrews 11:25). He laid aside his claim to fame and power to obey God's call and threw in his lot with a bunch of slaves. In the process he became one of the most famous and influential men who ever lived. He was the friend of God (Exodus 33:11) and the inspired author of the first five books of the Old Testament.

Read John 14:14–15.

Questions:

What does it mean to be a friend of God?

✎ _____

_____

How can this become a reality in your own life?

✎ _____

_____

Word Wealth—*Looked*

Looked: Greek *apoblepo* (ap-ob-lep′-oh); Strong's #578: *Apoblepo* is a graphic word that combines *apo*, meaning "away from," and *blepo*, meaning "to see." The word literally means "to look away from everything else in order to look intently on one object." Moses looked away from the wealth of the world systems toward a messianic future.

Probing the Depths

The Hebrew Christians who received this epistle were experiencing conflict because of their faith in Jesus. It was uncertain whether they would experience victory over their persecutors. In fact it was much more likely that the persecution would continue indefinitely.

That others were tortured and suffered in various other ways indicates that faith does not provide an automatic exemption from hardship, trials, or tragedy. Furthermore, the experience of such difficulties does not mean that the people undergoing them possess less faith than those who are not afflicted. The same faith that enables some to escape trouble enables others to endure it. The same faith that delivers some from death enables others to die victoriously.

Faith is not a bridge over troubled waters but is a pathway through them. Discerning the pathway and the source of any hardships encountered requires aggressive prayer and worship. Through these means God's perspective becomes focused.

Read Isaiah 43:1–3; John 16:33.

Questions:

What is the purpose of trial and hardship in the life of a Christian?

_____

_____

In what ways has your faith been tested through trial?

_____

_____

What was your reaction?

_____

_____

What has been the resulting benefit in your life?

✎_____

_____

Record Your Thoughts

Questions:

How can your faith in Christ—who is the best object of faith—sustain you through times of persecution?

✎_____

_____

What worldly attitudes do you need to deal with to give your faith freedom to resist persecution?

✎_____

_____

Whom have you known to be a person of such faith that "the world was not worthy" (Hebrews 11:38) of him or her? How did he or she show this faith?

✎_____

_____

How are faith in the person of Christ and faith in the promises of God related to each other?

✎_____

_____

How has your faith in Christ already given you victory over sin, death, and the world?

✎_____

_____

What do you need to look away from in order to keep looking in faith toward the Lord Jesus and the Word of God?

✎_____

_____

SESSION ELEVEN

The Best Example

Hebrews 12:1–29

Kingdom Key—*Imitate Christ*

1 Peter 2:21–24 To this you were called, because Christ also suffered for us, leaving us an example, that you should follow His steps: "Who committed no sin, nor was deceit found in His mouth"; who, when He was reviled, did not revile in return; when He suffered, He did not threaten, but committed Himself to Him who judges righteously; who Himself bore our sins in His own body on the tree, that we, having died to sins, might live for righteousness—by whose stripes you were healed.

The writer of Hebrews held up Jesus as the example for the Hebrew Christians to follow as they tried to decide how to handle the hostility they were experiencing because of their faith. The Hebrews needed maturity in their imitation of Jesus.

We must live godly lives, even in the midst of trial, suffering, or persecution. Circumstances do not affect godly principles for living. Whether you are being loved or cursed, you are to bless. Whether you will be embraced or persecuted, your life and testimony are to witness to the hope of salvation in Jesus Christ. Consistency in godly living, despite circumstances, is the true test of growth in Christlikeness.

We must understand that suffering is a part of the Christian life. To walk in stable, consistent faith, we must look to Jesus' responses to suffering and follow His example.

Read Romans 6:4–14; Ephesians 5:1–2; Colossians 3:12–17.

Questions:

In what ways are your relationships affected by negative circumstances in your life?

In what ways is your faith affected by negative circumstances?

✎_____

_____

In what ways do you fail to show forth Christlikeness in the midst of trial?

✎_____

_____

What steps can you take to more consistently and effectively live out your faith and represent Jesus to the world?

✎_____

_____

Probing the Depths

Hebrews 12:1 contains wording that is easily and often misunderstood. The "cloud of witnesses" that surrounds us is not to be understood as a group of heroes of the faith watching as the spectators of our lives. Rather, their lives are witnesses to us. Their lives teach us, guide us, and give us hope as we are reminded of their success in overcoming the world.

To imitate them we must lay aside anything that hinders our progress, particularly every form of sin.

As a runner must remain focused on the race, so we must remain focused on the upward call of God. As a runner must focus on the goal and not on other contestants, so we must ever keep our eyes fixed on Jesus.

Read 1 Corinthians 9:24–27; 2 Corinthians 10:4–5; Philippians 3:12–14.

Questions:

What are the things in your life that hinder your walk of faith?

✎_____

_____

_____

How can you effectively fight against these things?

_____

_____

Behind the Scenes

The disciple is an apprentice to Jesus, learning to live as He did. Discard any attitude or practice that hinders your walk with Christ. Model your life after Jesus and develop a dynamic discipleship. Give careful thought and study to the life of Jesus for encouragement in your struggle with sin. Embrace God's discipline. Know that it is evidence that He is training you as His child. Accept God's correction as necessary for spiritual growth.

Kingdom Life—*Accept Discipline*

The readers must not assume that the sufferings they are enduring as a result of their Christian profession mean that God is unconcerned about their welfare. Far from neglecting them, He shows Himself to be a true Father in the experience of discipline.

"Chastening" (Hebrews 12:7) describes corrective discipline used in training a child. Such treatment is administered not harshly, but in love, with the well-being of the child in mind. Instead of becoming discouraged, the readers should view their persecutions as evidence of God's love for them as His children, bringing them to spiritual maturity.

The writer of Hebrews does not suggest that God is responsible for the sufferings that hostile sinners bring upon them, but he does indicate that God uses even adverse circumstances as instruments to accomplish His purpose.

Read Proverbs 3:11–12; Revelation 3:19.

Questions:

Have you ever felt chastened by God?

_____

_____

What lessons did you learn from those circumstances?

✎ _____

_____

_____

Kingdom Life—*Develop Spiritual Strength*

Before you can follow the example of Jesus successfully for any length of time, you need to build up your spiritual vitality and purity. A lot of fans watch sporting contests religiously and imagine performing the feats their favorite players do, but in reality they are in no physical condition to do any of it. Spiritually, we can marvel at the grace and truth of Jesus and not have the spiritual conditioning to imitate Him.

Read 1 Corinthians 13:11–12; Galatians 5:16–26; James 5:16.

Questions:

What practical steps could you take to strengthen your Christian life?

✎ _____

_____

_____

What practical steps can you take to assist your Christian brothers and sisters to become stronger saints?

✎ _____

_____

_____

Behind the Scenes

Esau was a son of Isaac and Rebekah and the twin brother of Jacob. Esau was born first. By Old Testament custom he would have inherited most of his father's property and the right to succeed him as family patriarch. But in a foolish, impulsive moment, he sold his birthright to Jacob in exchange for a meal (Genesis 25:29–34).

Esau in many ways was more honest and dependable than his scheming brother Jacob. But he sinned greatly by treating his birthright so casually and selling it for a meal. To the ancient Hebrews one's birthright actually represented a high spiritual value. But Esau did not have the faith and farsightedness to accept this privilege and responsibility. Thus, the right passed by default to his younger brother.

The fate of Esau serves as a solemn warning to anyone who forfeits permanent spiritual blessings for immediate passing fleshly gratification. Once such a choice is made and acted on, its consequences cannot be reversed, and the blessings that might have been realized are lost forever.

Read Genesis 25:29–34.

Questions:

What circumstance can you recall where your actions resulted in lost blessing?

_____

_____

_____

What lessons did you learn through this experience?

_____

_____

_____

In what way has this experience changed your life?

_____

_____

_____

Behind the Scenes

Everything Israel and Judah built up in generations of self-effort was an abomination to God, and He systematically gave over for destruction (Jeremiah 32:29–36) all they had accomplished by "the works of their own hands" (Jeremiah 1:16).

The message of their misconception speaks to us today, and the writer of Hebrews summarizes the shaking God is determined to perform (Hebrews 12:26–27). Everything built by the hand of man, in the energy and wisdom of the flesh, He has vowed to shake down. Only the things that cannot be shaken—the things built in His eternal power and wisdom—will remain.

The great shaking the author of Hebrews prophesied has begun and is continuing in the church today. For the same evils that plagued Israel—seeking to please God by external performance, lapsing into idolatry and moral decay, corruption in leadership, and worshipping the works of men's hands—are too present even in the church. Their removal is an essential part of the restoration process.

To the church as a whole, restoration means more than becoming a reproduction of the New Testament church. It means becoming all God originally intended the church to be. Remember, restoration means the establishment of something more and better than the original.

Record Your Thoughts

Questions:

Why is it important to revere the holiness and majesty of God while imitating and following Jesus?

_____

_____

_____

How can a sense of the majesty and terrible power of your holy God give you confidence to face opposition?

_____

_____

_____

What encouragement do you or could you derive from the witness of biblical heroes of faith and heroes of faith from church history?

_____

_____

_____

What disciplines do you need in order to become a better follower and imitator of Jesus?

Physically

_____

_____

_____

_____

Emotionally

_____

_____

_____

_____

Socially

_____

_____

_____

_____

Economically

_____

_____

_____

_____

Spiritually

_____

_____

_____

_____

ADDITIONAL OBSERVATIONS

The Best Aid

Hebrews 13:1–25

Kingdom Key—*Know the Shepherd*

John 10:14 I am the good shepherd; and I know My sheep, and am known by My own.

Jesus calls us His sheep, over which He is the "good shepherd." To understand this verse fully, we need to have a better understanding of the character of sheep and the nature of a shepherd's job.

Sheep are creatures of habit. They will continue to follow a known path rather than attempt to locate a better one. They are sometimes timid and sometimes stubborn, sometimes frightful and sometimes immovable. Sheep are quite helpless and defenseless. Sheep need a shepherd.

In order to understand the shepherd analogy, we must look to the ancient profession of sheepherding. In ancient times a shepherd's flock was small enough for him to be personally involved in the care of each one. He knew each sheep and often named each one. (Conversely, the sheep recognized the shepherd's voice and would follow wherever he led.) At night the shepherd would enclose his flock inside a fence made of rocks. The shepherd would place himself within the only opening into this enclosure, thus ensuring the safety of his flock.

Read Psalm 23; John 10:27–28.

Questions:

With this in mind, list the ways in which Jesus fulfills the role of good shepherd in your life.

Do you recognize His voice?

_____

_____

How might you increase your ability to hear and recognize Him?

_____

_____

_____

Kingdom Extra

"Brotherly love" translates the Greek word *philidelphia* (which is why Philadelphia, Pennsylvania, is called "the City of Brotherly Love"). The Greek term is compounded from *phileo,* meaning "to love," and *adelphos,* meaning "brother." The love denoted by *phileo* is affection based on natural attraction. The brotherhood created by faith in Jesus as Savior and Lord should bind believer to believer in warm, affectionate friendships based on Jesus' name.

Read John 13:34–35; 15:9–17; Romans 12:9–10.

Questions:

In what ways do you live out *phileo* in your life?

_____

_____

_____

What circumstances cause you to fail to respond in love?

_____

_____

_____

What steps can you take to increase brotherly love in your life?

_____

_____

_____

Behind the Scenes

Imprisonment in biblical times differed in purpose from imprisonment in modern Western societies. Imprisonment was not used as punishment for criminal behavior. Various forms of harsh corporal punishment typically punished crimes. In a few cases imprisonment removed troublesome people from society because civil authorities found their opinions or presence created social unrest. Long-term prisoners were, therefore, usually prisoners of conscience (for example, John the Baptist).

The vast majority of prisoners were being detained prior to trial or punishment (for example, Peter in Acts 12 and Paul and Silas in Acts 16). A debtor might be imprisoned until he was sold as a slave in order to pay his debts (Matthew 18:25, 30).

Imprisoned Christians, therefore, were probably short-term detainees in primitive dungeons or cells (Acts 12:6; 16:24) facing trial and physical punishment. They might need clothing (2 Timothy 4:13), medical attention, and better food as well as personal and spiritual support.

Word Wealth—*Helper*

Helper: Greek *boethos* (bah-ay-thoss′); Strong's #*998*: From *boe*, meaning "a cry for help," and *theo*, meaning "to run." *Boethos* is one who comes running when we cry for help. The word describes the Lord as poised and ready to rush to the relief of His oppressed children when they shout for His assistance.

Kingdom Life—*We Have Ever-Present Help*

In a world that seems immersed in materialism and the drive for financial gain, covetousness and financial fear run rampant. Even those who profess Jesus as Lord are seemingly drawn into this web of greed and gain.

But we have a promise from our Lord: "I will never leave you nor forsake you" (Hebrews 13:5). He assures us that He will be ever-present at the throne of God-making intercession on our behalf. Covetousness and financial fear are overcome by a contentment founded on the assurance of His constant help and the promises He extends to us to supply our daily needs. Because we have His assurance, we may boldly respond with a declaration of confidence in the face of any need.

Read Psalms 9:8–9; 46:1–3; Luke 12:27–31.

Questions:

What has been your reaction in the past when faced with a seemingly impossible need?

_____

_____

What has your past reaction spoken of your faith?

_____

_____

Probing the Depths

Why is praising God a sacrifice? The word *sacrifice* (Greek *thusia*) comes from the root *thuo,* a verb meaning "to kill or slaughter for a purpose." Praise often requires that we kill our pride, fear, or sloth—anything that threatens to diminish or interfere with our worship of the Lord.

We also discover here the basis of all our praise: the sacrifice of our Lord Jesus Christ. It is by Him, in Him, with Him, to Him, and for Him that we offer our sacrifice of praise to God. Praise will never be successfully hindered when we keep its focus on Him, the Founder and the Completer of our salvation. His cross, His blood—His love gift of life and forgiveness to us—keep praise as a *living* sacrifice!

Read Romans 12:1–2.

Questions:

Do you praise God even in the tough times? Why?

_____

_____

_____

In what ways do you fail to offer your life in sacrifice to the Lord?

What are some ways that you can worship the Lord with sacrifice?

Kingdom Life—*Complete in Him*

"Make you complete" translates an important biblical word (*katarizo*) that has as its basic meaning "to arrange everything in the proper order for the best effect." Greek medical literature applied this word to setting broken bones. In the Gospels it is used of fishermen repairing their nets (Matthew 4:21). It isn't necessary for something to be broken for it to be completed. In Hebrews 10:5 this word is used of the provision of a human body for Jesus. In Hebrews 13:21 the notion of the verb seems to be the harmonious application of all the truth about the new covenant—all that Christ died to provide and lives (seated at the right hand of God) to make real for His followers.

Read Romans 8:34; Colossians 2:9.

Questions:

In what ways do you fail to be "complete in every good work" (Hebrews 13:21)?

How might this failure be overcome?

How might you be enabled to apply God's truth to your life more fully?

✎ ....

....

Jesus is at God's right hand, making intercession for you. What impact does this fact have on your ability and determination to be "complete in every good work"?

✎ ....

....

....

Record Your Thoughts

Questions:

At this point in time, what is the major focus of your life? Honestly, what has most of your time and attention?

✎ ....

....

....

How does this fact affect your walk with the Lord?

✎ ....

....

....

What area of your spiritual life would you like the Great Shepherd of the sheep to bring into balanced and completed shape? Why?

✎ ....

....

....

What steps can you take to enhance your relationship with the Lord and begin to become the mature believer God means for you to be?

✎ ....

....

Conclusion

Before Jesus, the presence of God was hidden "behind the veil" (Hebrews 6:19). Sin created a barrier between God and man that could not be crossed—until the cross. Jesus has opened the way for us to enter into the very presence of God. The veil that once separated us from His presence was torn in two (Matthew 27:51). Jesus' death paid the penalty for our sin, and we can now come boldly, as precious children, into the very throne room of God.

We are now free to live like Jesus. By the power of the Holy Spirit, we can walk in freedom and live in His glorious presence.

Probing the Depths—*Review*

The book of Hebrews has given us much insight into the manifold grace of God and all that has been bestowed upon us as a result of Christ's sacrifice. The recognition of these truths and the application of their power in our lives will enable us to be true emissaries for our Lord.

Let's review these truths and consider how each will impact our own lives and the lives of those around us. As you read each Kingdom Key, try to recall what that session spoke to you regarding your relationship and walk with the Lord.

1. **Behold Him**

_____

_____

_____

2. **Find Peace with God**

_____

_____

_____

3. **Know God's Supply**

_____

_____

_____

4. Embrace Understanding

_____

_____

5. Come to the Father

_____

_____

6. Believe God

_____

_____

7. Be Purified

_____

_____

8. You Are Justified

_____

_____

9. Have Confident Hope

_____

_____

10. Only Believe

_____

_____

11. Imitate Christ

_____

_____

12. Know the Shepherd

_____

_____

You are able to pursue holiness in your daily life because you have been made holy through the perfect sacrifice of Jesus. He gave Himself, once for all, for the forgiveness of sin. His sacrifice was final; nothing else is necessary. Jesus' sacrifice made you holy and opened the way for you to enter the very presence of Holy God, your Father. You can freely enter God's presence; you can serve Him faithfully and with great power, bringing Him honor in all that you do.

Grace be with you all. Amen (Hebrews 13:25).

ADDITIONAL OBSERVATIONS